In "*Financial Empowerment: Unlocking Your Path to Wealth and Security*", you can discover the keys to mastering your personal finances and building a prosperous future. This comprehensive guide offers actionable strategies and expert advice on budgeting, saving, investing, and more. Take control of your financial journey and unlock the path to long-term wealth and security.

Theia Stewart
Member of PageTitans

Please don't forget to follow me on Amazon:

https://amazon.com/author/theiastewart

This book may not be copied, scanned, or distributed in any form, whether electronic or printed, without the prior written consent of the author.

We would greatly appreciate it if you could provide a review as we love to receive feedback from our customers. Thank you.

Financial Empowerment: Unlocking Your Path to Wealth and Security

Table of Contents

01. Create a budget to track income and expenses..1
02. Save a portion of your income regularly...4
03. Invest in diversified portfolios for long-term wealth growth..7
04. Educate yourself about personal finance through books and courses....................................10
05. Pay off high-interest debts to reduce financial burden...13
06. Start an emergency fund for unexpected expenses..16
07. Automate savings and investment contributions...19
08. Live below your means to save more money..22
09. Use credit cards responsibly and pay off balances in full each month..................................25
10. Take advantage of employer-sponsored retirement plans...28
11. Set specific financial goals and work towards achieving them..30
12. Avoid impulsive spending and practice mindful consumption..33
13. Develop multiple streams of income to increase earning potential......................................35
14. Negotiate better deals on purchases and services..37
15. Prioritize long-term value over short-term gains...40
16. Invest in your education and develop new skills for career growth.....................................43
17. Consider real estate investment opportunities..46
18. Regularly review and optimize your investment portfolio...50
19. Start a side business or freelancing gig for additional income..53
20. Protect yourself and your assets through insurance...56
21. Maximize tax-efficient savings and investment accounts..59
22. Leverage the power of compound interest by starting to invest early..................................62
23. Network and build relationships for career and financial opportunities...............................65
24. Learn about personal tax strategies to minimize tax liabilities..68
25. Take calculated risks in investment opportunities...72
26. Invest in yourself through personal development and self-improvement.............................75
27. Avoid unnecessary fees and charges by choosing low-cost financial products.....................77
28. Understand and manage your credit score effectively...80
29. Diversify your investments across different asset classes..82
30. Invest in index funds for broad market exposure and low fees...85
31. Stay informed about economic trends and market developments..88
32. Practice long-term thinking and avoid emotional investment decisions...............................90
33. Invest in your health and well-being for long-term cost savings...93
34. Create a will and establish an estate plan to protect your assets..95
35. Understand the power of compounding and the time value of money..................................97
36. Take steps to minimize investment fees and expenses...100
37. Automate bill payments to avoid late fees and penalties..102
38. Evaluate and adjust your investment strategy based on changing market conditions..........104
39. Teach children about money management and financial literacy......................................106
40. Seek professional advice for complex financial matters..108
41. Plan for retirement and set aside funds for post-work life..111
42. Continuously educate yourself about personal finance to make informed decisions...........113
Book references..117

Disclaimer: The information provided in this book is for informational purposes only and should not be considered financial or investment advice. The content presented is based on the author's research, knowledge, and personal experiences. However, every individual's financial situation is unique, and readers are encouraged to conduct their own thorough research and seek the advice of qualified professionals before making any personal or financial decisions.

The author and publisher of this book are not responsible for any errors, omissions, or inaccuracies in the information presented. The content is subject to change without notice and may not reflect the most current financial regulations or market conditions. The reader assumes full responsibility for any actions taken based on the information provided in this book.

It is important to recognize that investing and financial decisions involve inherent risks, and past performance is not indicative of future results. Readers should carefully consider their own financial goals, risk tolerance, and seek professional guidance before implementing any investment strategies or making significant financial commitments.

The author and publisher disclaim any liability or responsibility for any direct, indirect, or consequential loss or damage incurred by readers or third parties arising from the use or reliance on the information provided in this book.

It is recommended that readers consult with a qualified financial advisor, accountant, or attorney regarding their specific financial situation and goals. Each individual's financial circumstances are unique, and personalized advice should be sought to address specific needs.

By reading this book, the reader acknowledges and agrees to release the author and publisher from any liability or claims arising from the use or application of the information provided. The reader is solely responsible for their financial decisions and actions.

Please note that laws, regulations, and financial practices may vary by jurisdiction. It is the reader's responsibility to comply with applicable laws and regulations in their respective country or region.

Always exercise caution, prudence, and due diligence when it comes to managing your finances and investments.

01. Create a budget to track income and expenses.

By tracking income and expenses, a budget provides valuable insights, allowing individuals to make informed decisions, prioritize financial goals, and achieve personal economic growth. Now we will explore the significance of budgeting, its benefits, and practical steps to create an effective budget that can pave the way to success.

Understanding the Power of Budgeting: A budget serves as a roadmap, offering a comprehensive overview of your financial situation. It enables you to understand where your money is coming from, how it is being spent, and how it can be optimized to align with your goals. Here's why budgeting is crucial:

1. **Financial Awareness**: Creating a budget brings clarity to your finances. It provides a clear picture of your income, expenses, and savings, allowing you to identify areas where you can make adjustments and optimize your financial resources.

2. **Goal Setting**: A budget helps you set financial goals and work towards achieving them. Whether it's saving for a down payment on a house, starting a business, or planning for retirement, a budget allows you to allocate resources strategically and track progress towards your goals.

3. **Expense Management**: With a budget, you can gain better control over your spending habits. By tracking expenses, you can identify areas where you may be overspending and make conscious decisions to reduce unnecessary expenditures.

4. **Debt Management**: Budgeting plays a vital role in managing and paying off debts. It enables you to allocate funds towards debt repayment, prioritize high-interest debts, and develop a plan to become debt-free over time.

5. **Emergency Preparedness**: A well-structured budget accounts for unforeseen circumstances. By setting aside funds for emergencies, you create a safety net that protects you from unexpected financial setbacks.

Practical Steps to Create a Budget: Now, let's explore the practical steps to create a budget that will set you on the path to personal economic growth:

1. **Gather Financial Information**: Start by collecting information about your income sources, such as salaries, investments, or any other means of income. Additionally, compile details of your monthly expenses, including

rent or mortgage payments, utilities, groceries, transportation, and discretionary spending.

2. **Categorize Your Expenses**: Divide your expenses into categories to organize your budget effectively. Common categories include housing, transportation, utilities, groceries, debt payments, entertainment, and savings. Tailor the categories to suit your specific financial situation.

3. **Determine Income and Expense Amounts**: Calculate your total income and total expenses for a given period, usually monthly. Be thorough and include all sources of income and all types of expenses. This will provide a clear understanding of your financial inflows and outflows.

4. **Prioritize Financial Goals**: Identify your short-term and long-term financial goals. Whether it's saving for a dream vacation, paying off debt, or building an emergency fund, assign priorities to each goal based on its importance to you.

5. **Allocate Funds**: Assign specific amounts to each expense category based on your income and priorities. Ensure that essential expenses are covered first, followed by savings and debt repayments. Allocate remaining funds to discretionary categories, such as entertainment or hobbies.

6. **Track and Monitor**: Implement a system to track and monitor your expenses regularly. This can be done using a spreadsheet, budgeting apps, or dedicated budgeting software. Review your budget periodically to assess progress, make adjustments, and ensure that you are staying on track.

7. **Be Realistic and Flexible**: When creating a budget, be realistic about your income and expenses. Avoid overestimating income or underestimating expenses. Be flexible and willing to make adjustments as needed to accommodate unexpected changes or fluctuations in income or expenses.

8. **Seek Professional Guidance**: If you feel overwhelmed or need assistance, consider consulting a financial advisor. A professional can provide personalized guidance, help optimize your budget, and offer valuable insights into money management strategies.

Insights from Renowned Experts:

1. **Dave Ramsey**: Dave Ramsey, a well-known personal finance expert and author of "*The Total Money Makeover*". In this bestselling book, Dave Ramsey outlines a step-by-step plan for achieving financial freedom. He emphasizes the importance of budgeting as a foundational tool for

managing money effectively. Ramsey provides practical tips on creating a budget, tracking income and expenses, and setting financial goals.

2. **Elizabeth Warren**: Elizabeth Warren, a U.S. Senator and a prominent advocate for financial reform, stresses the significance of budgeting. In her book "*All Your Worth: The Ultimate Lifetime Money Plan*" co-authored with her daughter, **Amelia Warren Tyagi**, she provides practical advice on creating a balanced budget and achieving financial stability.

Other Book Examples:

1. "*You Need a Budget: The Proven System for Breaking the Paycheck-to-Paycheck Cycle, Getting Out of Debt, and Living the Life You Want*" by **Jesse Mecham**: Jesse Mecham, the founder of **You Need a Budget (YNAB)**, shares his proven budgeting system in this book. He guides readers on how to create a budget, allocate funds to different categories, and gain control over their finances. The book offers actionable strategies and real-life examples to help readers track income and expenses effectively.

2. "*The 30-Day Money Cleanse: Take Control of Your Finances, Manage Your Spending, and De-Stress Your Money for Good*" by **Ashley Feinstein Gerstley**: In this book, Ashley Feinstein Gerstley provides a 30-day plan to improve your financial well-being. She emphasizes the importance of creating a budget as the foundation of financial success. Gerstley offers practical exercises, tools, and resources to help readers track their income and expenses and make intentional financial decisions.

Practical Tips for Creating a Budget to Track Income and Expenses:

1. **Calculate Your Income**: Start by determining your total income, including salary, bonuses, freelance income, or any other sources of revenue.

2. **Track Your Expenses**: Record all your expenses for a certain period, such as a month, to get a clear understanding of where your money is going. Categorize your expenses into fixed expenses (e.g., rent, utilities) and variable expenses (e.g., groceries, entertainment).

3. **Set Financial Goals**: Define your financial goals, whether it's paying off debt, saving for a down payment, or building an emergency fund. Your budget should align with these goals and help you allocate funds accordingly.

4. **Differentiate Needs and Wants**: Differentiate between essential needs and discretionary wants. Prioritize your needs in your budget while being mindful of your wants.

5. **Allocate Funds to Categories**: Divide your income into different categories based on your expenses. This helps you allocate specific amounts for each category and ensure that you don't overspend.

6. **Monitor and Adjust**: Regularly track your expenses against your budget to identify any areas where you may be overspending. Make adjustments as needed to align your spending with your financial goals.

7. **Use Budgeting Tools and Apps**: Utilize budgeting tools and apps like Mint, You Need a Budget (YNAB), or Personal Capital to simplify the budgeting process and track your income and expenses effectively.

8. **Stay Disciplined**: Stick to your budget and avoid impulsive spending. Regularly review your budget to ensure you're on track and make adjustments when necessary.

Conclusion: Creating a budget is a fundamental step in managing your finances effectively. Insights from renowned experts like **Dave Ramsey** and **Elizabeth Warren**, as well as books such as "*The Total Money Makeover*", "*You Need a Budget*" and "*The 30-Day Money Cleanse*" provide valuable guidance on creating and following a budget. By tracking your income and expenses, setting financial goals, and making informed decisions, you can take control of your money and work towards a more secure financial future. Remember, consistency and discipline are key to successfully implementing a budget and achieving your financial objectives.

02. Save a portion of your income regularly.

One essential practice that paves the way to financial success is saving a portion of your income regularly. By cultivating the habit of saving, individuals can build a financial safety net, achieve their goals, and create a secure and prosperous future. We will explore the importance of regular saving, its benefits, and practical strategies to incorporate this practice into your life.

Understanding the Power of Regular Saving: Regular saving is a fundamental step towards personal economic growth and financial well-being. Here's why saving a portion of your income regularly is crucial:

1. **Financial Security**: Saving provides a safety net that protects you from unexpected expenses, emergencies, or periods of financial instability. It offers peace of mind, knowing that you have funds set aside to weather unforeseen circumstances.

2. **Goal Achievement**: Saving regularly allows you to work towards your financial goals, such as buying a house, starting a business, funding education, or planning for retirement. It empowers you to take control of your financial future and make progress towards your aspirations.

3. **Wealth Accumulation**: Regular saving is the foundation of building wealth. By consistently setting aside a portion of your income, you can accumulate capital over time, which can be invested wisely to generate further growth and financial opportunities.

4. **Flexibility and Freedom**: Having savings provides a sense of freedom and flexibility in making life choices. It gives you the ability to pursue new opportunities, change careers, or navigate through unexpected transitions without being solely reliant on paycheck-to-paycheck living.

Practical Strategies for Regular Saving: Now, let's explore practical strategies to incorporate regular saving into your life and maximize its impact:

1. **Set a Savings Target**: Determine a specific savings target that aligns with your financial goals. This could be a percentage of your income or a fixed amount. Start with an attainable target and gradually increase it as your income grows or expenses decrease.

2. **Pay Yourself First**: Treat saving as an essential expense and prioritize it by allocating a portion of your income towards savings right at the beginning of each month. Automate the process by setting up automatic transfers from your checking account to a dedicated savings account.

3. **Create a Budget**: Establishing a budget allows you to identify areas where you can reduce expenses and allocate more funds towards savings. Track your income and expenses, and make conscious decisions about your spending habits to free up additional resources for saving.

4. **Cut Unnecessary Expenses**: Review your expenses critically and identify areas where you can make cuts or adjustments. Evaluate discretionary spending, subscriptions, dining out, or impulse purchases. Redirect the money saved from these expenses into your savings.

5. **Embrace Frugality**: Practice mindful consumption and adopt a frugal mindset. Look for opportunities to save money without sacrificing quality

of life. Compare prices, buy in bulk, use coupons, and opt for cost-effective alternatives whenever possible.

6. **Reduce Debt**: Prioritize paying off high-interest debts, such as credit card balances or personal loans. As you reduce your debt burden, allocate the money previously used for debt payments towards savings. This accelerates your progress and frees up more funds for saving in the long run.

7. **Track Your Progress**: Regularly monitor your savings growth to stay motivated and track your progress. Celebrate milestones along the way to reinforce positive saving habits and keep your financial goals in focus.

8. **Increase Savings with Income Growth**: Whenever you receive a salary raise or bonus, resist the temptation to inflate your lifestyle immediately. Instead, increase your savings proportionally to capitalize on the additional income and expedite your financial growth.

9. **Review and Adjust**: Periodically review your savings strategy and make adjustments as needed. Changes in income, expenses, or financial goals may warrant modifications to your savings plan. Stay adaptable and proactive in optimizing your savings approach.

10. **Seek Professional Advice**: If you're unsure about financial matters or need guidance, consult a financial advisor. They can provide personalized advice, help you develop a comprehensive savings strategy, and offer insights on investment opportunities to further grow your wealth.

Insights from Renowned Experts:

1. **Warren Buffett**: Warren Buffett, one of the most successful investors in the world, stresses the importance of saving and investing. He advises individuals to save a portion of their income consistently and invest it wisely to build wealth over time.

2. **Suze Orman**: Suze Orman, a renowned personal finance expert and author of *"The Money Book for the Young, Fabulous & Broke"* emphasizes the significance of saving regularly. She believes that saving is crucial for financial security and recommends individuals prioritize saving before spending.

Other Book Examples:

1. *"The Automatic Millionaire: A Powerful One-Step Plan to Live and Finish Rich"* by **David Bach**: In this book, David Bach emphasizes the power of saving consistently. He introduces the concept of "paying yourself first,"

which involves automatically saving a portion of your income before allocating it to other expenses. Bach provides practical strategies and examples to help readers develop a saving habit.

2. "*I Will Teach You to Be Rich*" by **Ramit Sethi**: Ramit Sethi's book focuses on personal finance and offers a comprehensive plan for achieving financial success. He highlights the importance of saving regularly and automating the process to make it easier. Sethi provides actionable steps and tips on how to save, invest, and grow your wealth over time.

3. "*The Richest Man in Babylon*" by **George S. Clason**: Although an older book, "*The Richest Man in Babylon*" offers timeless financial wisdom. The book shares the story of characters who achieve wealth by saving a portion of their income regularly. It emphasizes the concept of "pay yourself first" and provides practical advice on managing money and building wealth.

Conclusion: Saving a portion of your income regularly is a powerful practice that can lead to personal economic growth, financial security, and the realization of your dreams. By prioritizing saving, setting goals, and adopting smart financial habits, you can build a solid foundation for a prosperous future. Remember, the journey of regular saving is a marathon, not a sprint. Stay committed, embrace discipline, and enjoy the incremental progress you make along the way. With each dollar saved, you are investing in your own success, both in business and in life.

03. Invest in diversified portfolios for long-term wealth growth.

One powerful strategy that can accelerate your financial journey is investing in diversified portfolios. By spreading your investments across various asset classes and sectors, you can mitigate risks, capture growth opportunities, and pave the way for long-term wealth accumulation. We will explore the importance of diversified portfolios, their benefits, and practical insights to help you embark on a successful investment journey.

Understanding the Power of Diversification: Diversification is the practice of spreading investments across different asset classes, such as stocks, bonds, real estate, and commodities, as well as various industries and geographic regions. Here's why investing in diversified portfolios is crucial for long-term wealth growth:

1. **Risk Mitigation**: Diversification helps reduce the impact of individual investment risks. By spreading your investments across different assets, industries, and regions, you can lower the overall risk associated with any

single investment. This ensures that the potential losses from one investment are balanced by gains from others, safeguarding your portfolio against significant downturns.

2. **Capture Growth Opportunities**: Diversified portfolios enable you to participate in a wide range of investment opportunities. Different asset classes and sectors may perform differently at different times. By having exposure to various investments, you increase the likelihood of benefiting from sectors or assets that are performing well, thereby enhancing your overall portfolio performance.

3. **Long-Term Wealth Accumulation**: Investing in diversified portfolios is a long-term wealth-building strategy. Over time, the power of compounding, combined with the potential growth from different assets, can generate substantial returns. By staying invested and maintaining a diversified approach, you give your investments the opportunity to grow and compound over the long run.

4. **Flexibility and Adaptability**: Diversification allows you to adapt to changing market conditions and economic cycles. By spreading your investments across different assets and sectors, you can adjust your portfolio in response to market trends, technological advancements, or geopolitical developments. This flexibility helps you navigate through uncertainties and take advantage of emerging opportunities.

Practical Insights for Investing in Diversified Portfolios: Now, let's explore practical insights to help you invest in diversified portfolios and unlock long-term wealth growth:

1. **Define Your Investment Goals**: Start by clarifying your investment objectives. Are you aiming for long-term growth, capital preservation, or income generation? Understanding your goals will guide your asset allocation and investment strategy.

2. **Determine Your Risk Tolerance**: Assess your risk tolerance by considering factors such as your time horizon, financial obligations, and comfort level with volatility. This will influence the balance between conservative and growth-oriented investments within your portfolio.

3. **Asset Allocation**: Allocate your investments across different asset classes based on your goals and risk tolerance. Common asset classes include stocks, bonds, real estate, and commodities. Consider diversifying within each asset class as well (e.g., different sectors within stocks).

4. **Geographic Diversification**: Expand your portfolio's reach by investing in various geographic regions. This diversifies your exposure to different economies, currencies, and geopolitical factors. Consider international funds or exchange-traded funds (ETFs) to access global markets.

5. **Regularly Rebalance Your Portfolio**: Periodically review your portfolio's allocation and rebalance it if necessary. As certain investments outperform or underperform, rebalancing ensures that your portfolio stays aligned with your desired asset allocation and risk profile.

6. **Consider Mutual Funds and ETFs**: Mutual funds and ETFs offer diversification benefits as they typically hold a basket of different securities. These investment vehicles provide exposure to a wide range of assets, making it easier to achieve diversification with a single investment.

7. **Seek Professional Advice**: If you're new to investing or unsure about constructing a diversified portfolio, consider consulting a financial advisor. They can provide personalized guidance, recommend suitable investments, and help you navigate the complexities of diversification.

8. **Monitor and Stay Informed**: Keep yourself updated on market trends, economic indicators, and the performance of your investments. Stay informed about the industries and sectors in which you have exposure. This knowledge will empower you to make informed investment decisions and capitalize on opportunities.

9. **Stay Disciplined and Patient**: Investing in diversified portfolios requires discipline and a long-term perspective. Stay focused on your investment strategy, resist the temptation to make impulsive decisions based on short-term market fluctuations, and remain patient as you allow your investments to grow over time.

Insights from Renowned Experts:

1. **Warren Buffett**: Warren Buffett, often referred to as the "Oracle of Omaha," is a renowned investor and the chairman and CEO of Berkshire Hathaway. Buffett advocates for investing in diversified portfolios. He emphasizes the importance of spreading investments across different asset classes to reduce risk and maximize long-term returns.

2. **Jack Bogle**: Jack Bogle, the founder of Vanguard Group and a pioneer in index fund investing, promoted the idea of diversification through low-cost index funds. Bogle believed that diversifying across a broad market index provides investors with exposure to the overall market performance and helps mitigate the risk associated with individual stock selection.

Book Examples:

1. "*The Intelligent Investor*" by **Benjamin Graham**: This classic investment book, written by Benjamin Graham, a renowned investor and mentor to Warren Buffett, highlights the significance of diversification. Graham advises investors to construct a diversified portfolio of stocks and bonds based on their risk tolerance and investment objectives. He emphasizes the need to avoid excessive concentration in a single investment or sector.

2. "*A Random Walk Down Wall Street*" by **Burton G. Malkiel**: In this influential book, Burton Malkiel promotes the concept of diversification through index fund investing. He argues that individual stock selection and market timing are difficult to consistently outperform the market. Malkiel advocates for investing in low-cost index funds that provide exposure to a diversified portfolio of stocks.

3. "*The Little Book of Common Sense Investing*" by **John C. Bogle**: Written by John C. Bogle, this book is a guide to long-term investing using index funds. Bogle emphasizes the importance of diversification and recommends investors focus on low-cost index funds that track broad market indices. He argues that maintaining a diversified portfolio and keeping investment costs low are key to achieving long-term wealth growth.

Conclusion: Investing in diversified portfolios is a powerful tool for personal economic growth, financial security, and long-term wealth accumulation. By spreading your investments across different asset classes, industries, and geographic regions, you can minimize risk, capture growth opportunities, and adapt to changing market conditions. Remember, building a diversified portfolio requires thoughtful planning, regular monitoring, and a disciplined approach. Embrace the potential of diversified investing, stay committed to your long-term goals, and enjoy the journey towards financial success in both business and life.

04. Educate yourself about personal finance through books and courses.

One powerful avenue for acquiring the knowledge and skills necessary to navigate the complex world of personal finance is through education. By immersing yourself in books and courses dedicated to personal finance, you can gain valuable insights, develop a solid financial foundation, and make informed decisions that will propel you towards success. We will explore the significance of financial education, its benefits, and practical tips for expanding your financial knowledge.

The Power of Financial Education: Financial education equips individuals with the knowledge and understanding needed to manage their personal finances effectively. Here's why educating yourself about personal finance is crucial:

1. **Building a Strong Foundation**: Financial education provides the groundwork for making sound financial decisions. By understanding key concepts such as budgeting, saving, investing, debt management, and retirement planning, you can establish a strong foundation for your personal economic growth.

2. **Empowering Decision-Making**: Education enables you to make informed decisions about your money. By learning about various financial instruments, investment strategies, and risk management techniques, you can navigate the complexities of the financial landscape with confidence and make choices that align with your goals and values.

3. **Developing Financial Discipline**: Education fosters financial discipline by promoting responsible money management habits. As you learn about the importance of budgeting, tracking expenses, and setting financial goals, you become better equipped to make conscious choices that prioritize long-term financial well-being over short-term gratification.

4. **Overcoming Financial Challenges**: Financial education equips you with the tools to overcome financial challenges. Whether it's dealing with debt, managing unexpected expenses, or planning for major life events, having the knowledge to navigate these situations can help you overcome obstacles and secure a brighter financial future.

Practical Tips for Financial Education: Now, let's explore practical tips to help you educate yourself about personal finance and unlock your full financial potential:

1. **Read Widely**: Begin by exploring books dedicated to personal finance. Choose titles that cover a range of topics, including budgeting, investing, retirement planning, and wealth management. Popular books authored by financial experts, such as "*Rich Dad Poor Dad*" by **Robert Kiyosaki** or "*The Total Money Makeover*" by **Dave Ramsey**, can provide valuable insights and actionable advice.

2. **Explore Online Courses**: Online platforms offer a wealth of educational resources on personal finance. Look for reputable courses that cover essential topics such as financial planning, investment strategies, and tax

management. Websites like **Coursera**, **Udemy**, and **Khan Academy** offer a variety of courses taught by industry professionals.

3. **Attend Workshops and Seminars**: Stay informed about local workshops or seminars focused on personal finance. These events often feature industry experts who provide practical tips and strategies. Take advantage of these opportunities to learn from professionals and engage in discussions with like-minded individuals.

4. **Follow Personal Finance Blogs and Podcasts**: Subscribe to personal finance blogs and podcasts to receive regular updates and insights. These platforms often share real-life stories, expert opinions, and practical tips that can enrich your financial knowledge. Some popular blogs and podcasts include **The Financial Diet**, **ChooseFI**, and **The Dave Ramsey Show**.

5. **Join Online Communities**: Engage with online communities dedicated to personal finance. Platforms like **Reddit**, **Quora**, and financial forums allow you to connect with others who share similar financial goals and challenges. Participate in discussions, seek advice, and learn from the experiences of others.

6. **Seek Professional Advice**: Consider consulting a financial advisor to receive personalized guidance. A qualified advisor can review your financial situation, help you set realistic goals, and provide tailored advice based on your unique circumstances. They can also recommend educational resources and strategies to maximize your financial growth.

7. **Apply Practical Knowledge**: As you gain knowledge through books and courses, actively apply what you learn to your own financial situation. Create a budget, track your expenses, set financial goals, and develop an investment plan. Putting theory into practice will enhance your understanding and improve your financial management skills.

Insights from Renowned Experts:

1. **Robert Kiyosaki**: Robert Kiyosaki, author of the bestselling book "*Rich Dad Poor Dad*" emphasizes the importance of financial education. He believes that learning about personal finance is crucial for building wealth and achieving financial independence. Kiyosaki encourages individuals to educate themselves through books, courses, and seminars to improve their financial knowledge.

2. **Dave Ramsey**: Dave Ramsey, a well-known personal finance expert and author of "*The Total Money Makeover*" stresses the significance of

financial literacy. He advises individuals to educate themselves about personal finance to make informed decisions and take control of their money. Ramsey's books and courses provide practical guidance on budgeting, debt management, and wealth building.

Other Book Examples:

1. "*The Millionaire Next Door*" by **Thomas J. Stanley** and **William D. Danko**: This book explores the characteristics and habits of wealthy individuals in America. It emphasizes the importance of financial education and highlights that many millionaires are self-educated and have a deep understanding of personal finance. The authors provide insights into the mindset and strategies of financially successful individuals.

2. "*Personal Finance for Dummies*" by **Eric Tyson**: As part of the popular "For Dummies" series, this book offers a comprehensive guide to personal finance. It covers a wide range of topics, including budgeting, saving, investing, and retirement planning. The book provides practical advice and insights for beginners, making it an excellent resource for financial education.

3. "*The Intelligent Investor*" by **Benjamin Graham**: While primarily focused on investing, this classic book by Benjamin Graham emphasizes the importance of financial education and the need for individuals to understand the fundamentals of investing. It provides valuable insights into investment strategies, risk management, and the psychology of the market.

Conclusion: Education is the key to unlocking personal economic growth, financial empowerment, and success in both business and life. By educating yourself about personal finance through books, courses, and other educational resources, you can build a strong financial foundation, make informed decisions, and navigate the complexities of the financial world with confidence. Remember, financial education is a continuous journey. Stay curious, embrace lifelong learning, and apply your knowledge to achieve your financial goals. With each step forward, you'll be better equipped to win in business and in life.

05. Pay off high-interest debts to reduce financial burden.

To triumph in both business and life, personal economic growth and financial freedom play vital roles. One powerful strategy to achieve this is by paying off high-interest debts, which can alleviate the financial burden and set you on the path to long-term success. We will delve into the significance of paying off high-interest debts, the benefits it brings, and practical steps you can take to reduce your financial burden.

Understanding the Impact of High-Interest Debts: High-interest debts, such as credit card balances, personal loans, or payday loans, can be detrimental to your financial well-being. Here's why paying off these debts is crucial:

1. **Reducing Financial Stress**: High-interest debts often come with hefty monthly payments, which can strain your budget and create financial stress. By paying off these debts, you free up your cash flow, allowing you to allocate your income towards other financial goals, investments, or emergency savings.

2. **Saving Money on Interest Payments**: High-interest debts accrue interest charges over time, making them more expensive in the long run. By paying off these debts early, you save money that would have otherwise gone towards interest payments. This can provide you with additional resources to invest, save, or enjoy the fruits of your labor.

3. **Improving Creditworthiness**: High levels of debt can negatively impact your credit score, which plays a crucial role in financial opportunities, such as obtaining loans or securing favorable interest rates. Paying off high-interest debts improves your credit utilization ratio, demonstrates financial responsibility, and enhances your overall creditworthiness.

4. **Building a Solid Financial Foundation**: Paying off high-interest debts sets the stage for long-term financial success. By eliminating these financial obligations, you gain the freedom to focus on building wealth, saving for retirement, or investing in opportunities that align with your goals.

Practical Steps to Pay Off High-Interest Debts: Now, let's explore practical steps you can take to pay off high-interest debts and reduce your financial burden:

1. **Assess Your Debt Situation**: Begin by gathering information about your debts, including outstanding balances, interest rates, and minimum monthly payments. This assessment provides a clear overview of your financial obligations, allowing you to prioritize which debts to tackle first.

2. **Create a Debt Repayment Plan**: Develop a comprehensive debt repayment plan that outlines your strategy for paying off high-interest debts. There are two popular approaches: the "Debt Snowball" method, where you start by paying off the smallest debt first, and the "Debt Avalanche" method, where you prioritize debts with the highest interest

rates. Choose the method that aligns best with your preferences and motivates you to stay on track.

3. **Cut Unnecessary Expenses**: Review your monthly expenses and identify areas where you can cut back. Consider reducing discretionary spending, renegotiating bills or subscriptions, and avoiding unnecessary purchases. Redirect the money saved towards your debt repayment plan, accelerating your progress.

4. **Increase Your Income**: Explore opportunities to boost your income. This can involve negotiating a salary raise, taking on a side job or freelance work, or starting a small business. The additional income can be allocated directly towards paying off high-interest debts, expediting your journey to financial freedom.

5. **Consider Debt Consolidation**: If you have multiple high-interest debts, consolidating them into a single loan with a lower interest rate can be beneficial. This simplifies your repayment process and reduces the overall interest you'll pay. However, carefully evaluate the terms and fees associated with debt consolidation before pursuing this option.

6. **Negotiate Lower Interest Rates**: Contact your creditors to inquire about the possibility of reducing your interest rates. In some cases, they may be willing to negotiate, especially if you have a history of timely payments. Lower interest rates can significantly decrease the total amount you'll repay and expedite your debt payoff journey.

7. **Seek Professional Assistance**: If you find yourself overwhelmed or struggling to develop a debt repayment plan, consider seeking assistance from a credit counseling agency. These professionals can provide guidance, negotiate with creditors on your behalf, and help you develop a personalized plan to pay off your high-interest debts.

Insights from Renowned Experts:

1. **Clark Howard**: Clark Howard, a renowned consumer expert and author, emphasizes the importance of paying off high-interest debts. He encourages individuals to prioritize debt repayment to reduce the financial burden and save on interest payments. Howard believes that being debt-free is essential for achieving financial stability and recommends developing a strategy to pay off high-interest debts as quickly as possible.

2. **Jean Chatzky**: Jean Chatzky, a well-known financial journalist and author, emphasizes the significance of paying off high-interest debts to improve financial well-being. She advises individuals to focus on eliminating high-

interest debts, such as credit card debt, as a priority. Chatzky provides practical guidance on debt reduction strategies and encourages readers to make informed financial decisions to regain control over their financial lives.

Book Examples:

1. *"Get Out of Debt, Stay Out of Debt, and Live Prosperously"* by **Jerrold Mundis**: This book by Jerrold Mundis provides practical advice and strategies for getting out of debt. Mundis addresses the issue of high-interest debts and offers insights into managing money, changing spending habits, and creating a debt repayment plan. The book provides motivation and guidance for individuals looking to reduce their financial burden.

2. *"Debt-Free: 9 Step System to Get Out of Debt Fast and Have Financial Freedom"* by **Ashton Pereira**: Ashton Pereira's book focuses on providing a step-by-step system for becoming debt-free. Pereira emphasizes the importance of paying off high-interest debts and offers practical strategies for debt reduction. The book provides readers with actionable tips and tools to tackle their debts and achieve financial freedom.

Conclusion: Paying off high-interest debts is a transformative step towards personal economic growth, financial liberation, and success in both business and life. By reducing your financial burden, you free up resources to invest, save, and pursue your dreams. Embrace the journey of debt repayment, develop a solid plan, and stay committed to your financial goals. As you pay off high-interest debts, you'll witness the positive impact on your financial well-being, empowering you to win in business and in life.

06. Start an emergency fund for unexpected expenses.

This financial safety net serves as a shield against unexpected expenses and provides peace of mind, allowing you to navigate challenges confidently. Now we will explore the importance of starting an emergency fund, its benefits, and practical steps you can take to build one for yourself.

Understanding the Significance of an Emergency Fund: An emergency fund is a designated pool of money set aside to cover unforeseen expenses. Here's why starting an emergency fund is crucial:

1. **Mitigating Financial Stress**: Unexpected expenses, such as medical bills, car repairs, or job loss, can cause immense financial stress. Having an

emergency fund in place provides a buffer, ensuring that you have funds readily available to address these situations without resorting to high-interest debt or depleting other savings.

2. **Protecting Long-Term Financial Goals**: An emergency fund safeguards your progress towards long-term financial goals. Without an emergency fund, you may be forced to tap into investments, retirement savings, or other planned allocations, derailing your financial journey. By having a separate fund for emergencies, you can protect your financial aspirations and stay on track.

3. **Minimizing Debt**: Unexpected expenses often lead to accumulating debt when individuals lack the necessary funds to cover them. Relying on credit cards or loans can result in high-interest charges and increased financial strain. An emergency fund acts as a financial safety net, allowing you to avoid debt or minimize its impact.

4. **Building Financial Resilience**: By creating an emergency fund, you cultivate financial resilience. It instills a sense of confidence and empowers you to face unexpected circumstances without compromising your overall financial stability. This resilience extends to both personal and professional realms, enabling you to navigate challenges and seize opportunities with greater ease.

Practical Steps to Start an Emergency Fund: Now, let's explore practical steps you can take to start an emergency fund and safeguard your financial well-being:

1. **Set Clear Savings Goals**: Determine how much you want to save for your emergency fund. Aim for a target amount that covers three to six months' worth of essential living expenses. This ensures you have a sufficient cushion to weather unexpected financial storms.

2. **Create a Budget**: Develop a comprehensive budget that outlines your income, expenses, and savings targets. Identify areas where you can trim discretionary spending and allocate the saved funds towards your emergency fund. A budget acts as a roadmap, helping you stay disciplined and focused on your financial goals.

3. **Automate Savings**: Make saving for your emergency fund effortless by automating the process. Set up an automatic transfer from your checking account to a separate savings account dedicated solely to emergency funds. This ensures consistent contributions without the temptation to divert the money elsewhere.

4. **Start Small and Increase Contributions**: If saving a substantial amount initially seems challenging, start with smaller contributions and gradually increase them over time. The key is to establish the habit of regular saving and make it a priority in your financial journey.

5. **Trim Unnecessary Expenses**: Assess your expenses and identify areas where you can cut back. Review subscriptions, dining out habits, entertainment expenses, or other discretionary spending. Redirecting the saved money towards your emergency fund can accelerate its growth.

6. **Generate Additional Income**: Explore opportunities to boost your income and expedite your emergency fund growth. Consider taking on a side job, freelancing, or monetizing a skill or hobby. The additional income can provide a significant boost to your savings efforts.

7. **Consider High-Yield Savings Accounts**: Look for high-yield savings accounts that offer competitive interest rates. These accounts allow your emergency fund to grow over time through compounded interest, maximizing its potential.

8. **Resist Temptation**: It's important to view your emergency fund as off-limits for non-emergency expenses. Resist the temptation to dip into it for non-essential purchases or vacations. Maintaining the integrity of your emergency fund ensures its availability when truly needed.

9. **Revisit and Replenish**: Regularly reassess your emergency fund goals and adjust them as needed. Life circumstances and financial obligations may change, necessitating a reevaluation of the target amount. Additionally, if you withdraw funds from the emergency fund, make it a priority to replenish them as soon as possible.

Insights from Renowned Experts:

1. **Suze Orman**: Suze Orman, a renowned financial advisor and author, emphasizes the importance of starting an emergency fund. She believes that having a financial safety net is crucial to protect yourself from unexpected expenses and emergencies. Orman recommends individuals aim to save at least six months' worth of living expenses in their emergency fund.

2. **Robert Kiyosaki**: Robert Kiyosaki, author of the bestselling book "*Rich Dad Poor Dad*" also stresses the significance of building an emergency fund. He advises individuals to save a portion of their income regularly and allocate a portion of those savings to an emergency fund. Kiyosaki believes

that having a financial cushion provides peace of mind and helps individuals navigate unexpected financial challenges.

Other Book Examples:

1. "*The Total Money Makeover*" by **Dave Ramsey**: In his book, Dave Ramsey emphasizes the importance of starting an emergency fund as part of a comprehensive financial plan. He suggests individuals begin by saving a small amount each month and gradually build their emergency fund to cover three to six months of living expenses. Ramsey provides practical strategies for saving and managing emergency funds.

2. "*The Automatic Millionaire*" by **David Bach**: David Bach's book highlights the significance of automating savings, including building an emergency fund. Bach encourages readers to set up automatic transfers from their income to a separate account designated for emergencies. He emphasizes the habit of consistent savings and building a financial safety net for unexpected expenses.

Conclusion: Starting an emergency fund is a crucial step towards personal economic growth, financial security, and success in both business and life. It provides a safety net to protect you from unexpected expenses, minimizes financial stress, and safeguards your long-term goals. By following practical steps, setting clear savings goals, and staying disciplined, you can establish a robust emergency fund that empowers you to navigate unforeseen circumstances with confidence. Remember, the journey towards financial stability begins with the first step. Start your emergency fund today and pave the way for a brighter, more secure future.

07. Automate savings and investment contributions.

By setting up automatic transfers, you can effortlessly build wealth, grow your savings, and secure a prosperous future. We will explore the benefits of automating your financial contributions, practical steps to implement automation, and real-life examples of its impact.

Understanding the Power of Automation: Automating your savings and investment contributions offers numerous advantages and propels you towards achieving your financial goals. Here's why it's a game-changer:

1. **Consistency and Discipline**: Automation ensures a consistent approach to savings and investments. By setting up recurring transfers, you eliminate the risk of forgetting or delaying contributions. This fosters discipline and

cultivates a habit of regular saving, essential for long-term financial growth.

2. **Time Efficiency**: Automating your financial contributions saves you valuable time. Instead of manually managing transactions, you can set up the automation process once and let it work in the background. This allows you to focus on other aspects of your life and business while your wealth accumulates steadily.

3. **Psychological Benefits**: Automation removes the need for decision-making on every savings or investment contribution. It eliminates the temptation to divert funds for short-term desires or impulses. By removing the human element, automation helps you stay committed to your financial goals, avoiding emotional or impulsive decisions.

4. **Dollar-Cost Averaging**: Automated contributions enable you to benefit from the concept of dollar-cost averaging. By investing a fixed amount at regular intervals, you buy more shares when prices are low and fewer shares when prices are high. Over time, this strategy can potentially reduce the impact of market volatility and enhance your investment returns.

Practical Steps to Automate Your Savings and Investments: Now, let's delve into practical steps you can take to automate your financial contributions and pave the way for personal economic growth:

1. **Assess Your Financial Goals**: Start by defining your financial objectives, whether it's building an emergency fund, saving for a down payment on a house, or planning for retirement. Clearly identifying your goals helps determine the amount you need to automate.

2. **Set Up Automatic Transfers**: Contact your bank or financial institution to establish automatic transfers from your checking account to a separate savings or investment account. Specify the frequency and amount of the transfers to align with your financial goals. Ideally, aim for a significant portion of your income while ensuring it's manageable within your budget.

3. **Choose the Right Accounts**: Select appropriate savings and investment accounts that align with your goals. For short-term goals and emergency funds, consider high-yield savings accounts or money market accounts. For long-term goals like retirement or wealth-building, explore retirement accounts (e.g., 401(k) or IRA) or brokerage accounts. Seek professional advice if necessary to make informed decisions.

4. **Consider Employer-Sponsored Retirement Plans**: If your employer offers a retirement savings plan, such as a 401(k), take advantage of it.

Contribute the maximum amount possible, especially if your employer matches a portion of your contributions. Automating these contributions helps grow your retirement savings effortlessly while benefiting from potential tax advantages.

5. **Embrace Robo-Advisors**: Robo-advisors are digital platforms that use algorithms to manage your investments. They offer convenience and automation, making it easier to allocate your funds and diversify your portfolio. Robo-advisors typically provide a user-friendly interface, low fees, and personalized investment strategies based on your risk tolerance and goals.

6. **Monitor and Adjust**: While automation brings convenience, it's crucial to regularly review your automated contributions. Assess your progress towards your financial goals, monitor investment performance, and make adjustments as needed. Life circumstances may change, requiring modifications to your automated contributions to ensure they remain aligned with your objectives.

Insights from Renowned Experts:

1. **David Bach**: David Bach, author of "*The Automatic Millionaire*" emphasizes the power of automation in savings and investment contributions. He believes that automating these processes can help individuals develop a consistent savings habit and ensure that they consistently allocate funds towards their financial goals.

2. **Tony Robbins**: Tony Robbins, a renowned motivational speaker and author of "*Money: Master the Game*" encourages individuals to automate their savings and investment contributions. He emphasizes the importance of making saving and investing a priority and recommends setting up automatic transfers to designated savings and investment accounts.

Other Book Examples:

1. "*I Will Teach You to Be Rich*" by **Ramit Sethi**: Ramit Sethi's book emphasizes the importance of automating savings and investment contributions. He advises readers to set up automatic transfers from their income to designated savings accounts, retirement accounts, and investment accounts. Sethi believes that automation eliminates the need for willpower and makes saving and investing effortless.

2. "*The Wealthy Barber*" by **David Chilton**: In this book, David Chilton uses the story of a fictional barber to share financial wisdom. Chilton advocates for automating savings and investment contributions by setting up

automatic transfers or payroll deductions. He highlights the benefits of this approach, such as disciplined savings and the potential for long-term wealth accumulation.

Conclusion: Automating your savings and investment contributions is a powerful tool for personal economic growth, finance management, and achieving success in both business and life. By setting up automatic transfers, you establish consistency, save time, and maintain discipline in your financial journey. Whether it's saving for emergencies, retirement, or other financial goals, automation helps you build wealth effortlessly. Take the practical steps outlined in this article, align your contributions with your goals, and embrace the benefits of automation. Let the power of automation propel you towards financial success and secure a prosperous future.

08. Live below your means to save more money.

By adopting a lifestyle that prioritizes frugality and conscious spending, you can save more money, build wealth, and create a solid foundation for future success. So we will explore the significance of living below your means, practical tips for implementing this approach, and real-life examples that illustrate its impact.

Understanding the Power of Living Below Your Means: Living below your means refers to spending less than what you earn and consciously managing your expenses to create a financial surplus. Here are key reasons why embracing this mindset is a game-changer:

1. **Building a Strong Financial Foundation**: Living below your means allows you to save money and build a solid financial foundation. By consistently spending less than you earn, you create a surplus that can be directed towards emergency funds, investments, debt repayment, and other financial goals. This foundation provides stability and acts as a springboard for future economic growth.

2. **Minimizing Debt and Financial Stress**: By living below your means, you can avoid accumulating unnecessary debt. Debt, particularly high-interest debt, can be a significant burden, hindering your progress towards financial success. Living within your means helps you minimize the reliance on credit, reduce financial stress, and maintain control over your financial situation.

3. **Creating a Culture of Saving and Investing**: Living below your means cultivates a culture of saving and investing. It encourages you to be

intentional about your spending, prioritize savings, and allocate funds towards investments that generate long-term wealth. This mindset shift can transform your financial journey and pave the way for future opportunities.

Practical Tips for Living Below Your Means: Now, let's explore practical tips and strategies to help you embrace the mindset of living below your means and achieve personal economic growth:

1. **Track Your Expenses**: Start by tracking your expenses meticulously. Use budgeting apps or spreadsheets to record your income and categorize your expenditures. This practice will provide a clear picture of where your money is going and highlight areas where you can cut back.

2. **Create a Realistic Budget**: Develop a budget that aligns with your financial goals. Differentiate between needs and wants, and allocate your income accordingly. Be realistic about your expenses, leaving room for unforeseen circumstances while ensuring you maintain a surplus for savings.

3. **Prioritize Value-Based Spending**: Focus on spending money on things that align with your values and bring genuine happiness and fulfillment. Evaluate purchases based on their long-term impact rather than short-term gratification. This approach helps you make conscious spending decisions and avoid impulse purchases.

4. **Cut Back on Unnecessary Expenses**: Identify areas where you can cut back without sacrificing your quality of life. Look for recurring expenses that can be reduced or eliminated, such as subscriptions, dining out, entertainment, or excessive shopping. Redirect the saved money towards your savings or investment accounts.

5. **Embrace Frugal Habits**: Embrace frugality as a lifestyle choice. Seek cost-effective alternatives in various aspects of your life, such as cooking meals at home, using public transportation, buying second-hand items, or negotiating better deals on utilities and services. These small changes can add up significantly over time.

6. **Distinguish Between Assets and Liabilities**: Differentiate between assets and liabilities when making purchasing decisions. Assets are items that appreciate in value or generate income, such as real estate or investment vehicles. Liabilities are items that depreciate or have ongoing expenses, such as luxury goods or excessive car purchases. Prioritize investing in assets that contribute to your long-term financial growth.

7. **Avoid Lifestyle Inflation**: As your income increases, resist the temptation to inflate your lifestyle proportionately. Instead, continue living below your means and allocate the additional income towards savings, investments, or debt repayment. This approach accelerates your financial progress and prevents unnecessary financial strain.

Insights from Renowned Experts:

1. **Elizabeth Warren**: Elizabeth Warren, a prominent economist and U.S. Senator, emphasizes the importance of living below your means. She encourages individuals to spend less than they earn and avoid excessive consumer debt. Warren believes that by living within your means, you can save more money and build a stronger financial foundation.

2. **Vicki Robin**: Vicki Robin, co-author of the book "*Your Money or Your Life*" advocates for living below your means as a key principle of financial independence. She suggests individuals reassess their needs, prioritize value-based spending, and avoid unnecessary expenses. Robin believes that by embracing a frugal lifestyle, individuals can save more money and achieve financial freedom.

Other Book Examples:

1. "*The Millionaire Next Door*" by **Thomas J. Stanley** and **William D. Danko**: This book examines the characteristics and habits of millionaires in America. It emphasizes the importance of living below your means and avoiding excessive spending. Stanley and Danko demonstrate that many wealthy individuals accumulate wealth by practicing frugality and making conscious choices about their expenses.

2. "*The Simple Path to Wealth*" by **J.L. Collins**: J.L. Collins' book focuses on achieving financial independence and retiring early. He emphasizes the concept of living below your means as a fundamental principle for saving and investing. Collins encourages readers to assess their spending habits, cut unnecessary expenses, and prioritize saving to build wealth over time.

Conclusion: Living below your means is a powerful approach to personal economic growth, finance management, and overall success in both business and life. By adopting a mindset of conscious spending, prioritizing savings, and making intentional financial decisions, you can create a strong financial foundation, reduce debt, and build wealth for the future. Implement the practical tips outlined in this article, learn from real-life examples, and embark on a journey towards living a fulfilling and financially secure life. Remember, the path to personal economic growth starts with a simple decision to live below your means.

09. Use credit cards responsibly and pay off balances in full each month.

In today's world, credit cards have become an integral part of personal finance. When used responsibly, credit cards can be powerful tools for personal economic growth, finance management, and building a solid credit history. However, misusing credit cards can lead to financial pitfalls and debt accumulation. We will explore how to use credit cards responsibly, the benefits of doing so, and practical tips to ensure you pay off your balances in full each month.

Understanding Responsible Credit Card Usage: Using credit cards responsibly involves using them as a tool for convenience, rewards, and establishing a positive credit history, while avoiding excessive debt and high interest charges. Here are some reasons why responsible credit card usage is essential:

1. **Building and Improving Credit**: Credit cards provide an opportunity to establish and improve your credit history. Consistently paying off your credit card balances in full and on time demonstrates responsible financial behavior to credit bureaus, positively impacting your credit score. A good credit score opens doors to future financial opportunities, such as obtaining low-interest loans or qualifying for better insurance rates.

2. **Earning Rewards and Benefits**: Many credit cards offer rewards programs, such as cashback, travel points, or discounts on purchases. Responsible credit card usage allows you to take advantage of these benefits, maximizing the value of your spending. By paying off your balances in full each month, you avoid interest charges and truly benefit from the rewards and perks offered by your credit card issuer.

3. **Convenience and Consumer Protection**: Credit cards provide a convenient and secure method of payment. They offer protection against fraud, and in case of disputes with merchants, credit card companies often provide buyer protection. Responsible credit card usage allows you to enjoy the convenience and peace of mind that come with using this financial tool.

Tips for Using Credit Cards Responsibly: Now that we understand the importance of responsible credit card usage, let's explore practical tips to help you leverage the benefits while avoiding the pitfalls:

1. **Choose the Right Credit Card**: Research and select a credit card that aligns with your financial goals and spending habits. Consider factors such as interest rates, annual fees, rewards programs, and additional features that suit your needs. Compare different options and read the terms and conditions carefully before making a decision.

2. **Set a Budget and Track Expenses**: Establish a monthly budget and track your expenses diligently. Use budgeting apps or spreadsheets to monitor your spending and ensure that your credit card purchases align with your financial plan. Avoid overspending or charging more than you can comfortably pay off at the end of the billing cycle.

3. **Pay Balances in Full and On Time**: The key to responsible credit card usage is paying off your balances in full each month. This practice eliminates the accumulation of interest charges and helps you maintain control of your finances. Set up automatic payments or reminders to ensure you never miss a payment deadline.

4. **Monitor Your Credit Card Activity**: Regularly review your credit card statements to identify any unauthorized or suspicious transactions. Keep track of your spending to stay within your budget and promptly address any errors or discrepancies. Monitoring your credit card activity empowers you to detect and resolve issues promptly, protecting your financial well-being.

5. **Avoid Cash Advances and Excessive Debt**: Cash advances from credit cards often come with high fees and interest rates. It's best to avoid using your credit card for cash advances unless it's absolutely necessary. Additionally, refrain from carrying high balances on your credit cards, as this can lead to debt accumulation and financial strain.

6. **Use Credit Utilization Wisely**: Credit utilization refers to the percentage of your available credit that you use. It is advisable to keep your credit utilization ratio below 30% to maintain a healthy credit score. Paying off your balances in full each month helps you manage your credit utilization effectively.

7. **Be Mindful of Credit Card Rewards**: While credit card rewards can be enticing, don't let them lead you to overspend. Only make purchases that you would have made anyway and ensure they align with your budget. Treat rewards as a bonus rather than a justification for unnecessary spending.

Insights from Renowned Experts:

1. **Jean Chatzky**: Jean Chatzky, a renowned financial journalist and author, emphasizes the importance of using credit cards responsibly. She advises individuals to pay off credit card balances in full each month to avoid accumulating high-interest debt. Chatzky believes that responsible credit card usage can help individuals build a positive credit history and financial stability.

2. **Dave Ramsey**: Dave Ramsey, a well-known personal finance expert, shares a similar view on responsible credit card usage. He advises individuals to pay off credit card balances in full every month to avoid interest charges and debt. Ramsey encourages individuals to use credit cards as a tool for convenience and rewards but urges caution in avoiding excessive debt.

Book Examples:

1. "*The Money Book for the Young, Fabulous & Broke*" by **Suze Orman**: Suze Orman's book addresses the topic of credit card usage and debt management. She emphasizes the importance of paying off credit card balances in full each month to avoid interest charges. Orman provides practical guidance on responsible credit card usage and offers strategies for getting out of credit card debt.

2. "*Credit Card Nation*" by **Robert D. Manning**: Robert Manning's book delves into the societal impact of credit card debt and provides insights into responsible credit card usage. Manning advises individuals to pay off credit card balances in full each month to avoid falling into the debt trap. He explores the psychological and economic factors associated with credit card use and offers strategies for responsible credit card management.

Conclusion: Using credit cards responsibly is a valuable skill that can contribute to personal economic growth, finance management, and overall success in both business and life. By paying off your credit card balances in full each month, you can establish a positive credit history, earn rewards, and avoid unnecessary debt. Implement the practical tips outlined in this article, learn from real-life examples, and embark on a journey of responsible credit card usage. Remember, responsible credit card usage is not only about convenience and rewards but also about maintaining control of your financial well-being and securing a prosperous future.

10. Take advantage of employer-sponsored retirement plans.

Planning for a secure financial future is crucial for personal economic growth and overall success in both business and life. One powerful tool at your disposal is an employer-sponsored retirement plan. These plans, such as 401(k)s or pension schemes, provide individuals with an opportunity to save for retirement while benefiting from potential tax advantages and employer contributions. Now we will explore the importance of employer-sponsored retirement plans, the advantages they offer, and practical strategies to make the most of them.

Understanding the Value of Employer-Sponsored Retirement Plans: Employer-sponsored retirement plans play a vital role in personal economic growth for several reasons:

1. **Tax Advantages**: Contributions to retirement plans are often made with pre-tax dollars, meaning that the money is deducted from your income before taxes are applied. This reduces your taxable income, potentially lowering your overall tax liability. Additionally, many retirement plans offer tax-deferred growth, meaning you won't pay taxes on the investment earnings until you withdraw the funds in retirement when you may be in a lower tax bracket.

2. **Employer Contributions**: Many employers offer matching contributions to retirement plans as an employee benefit. This means that for every dollar you contribute, your employer will contribute a certain percentage, effectively doubling your savings. Employer matches are essentially free money and can significantly boost your retirement savings over time.

3. **Long-Term Wealth Accumulation**: By participating in an employer-sponsored retirement plan, you have the opportunity to accumulate wealth over the course of your working years. The contributions you make, combined with potential investment growth and employer matches, can compound over time, resulting in a substantial nest egg for your retirement years.

Tips for Maximizing Employer-Sponsored Retirement Plans: To fully leverage the benefits of employer-sponsored retirement plans, consider the following strategies:

1. **Enroll and Contribute Early**: If your employer offers a retirement plan, don't hesitate to enroll as soon as you're eligible. The earlier you start, the more time your contributions have to grow. Aim to contribute the maximum amount allowed, or at least contribute enough to take full advantage of your employer's matching contributions.

2. **Understand the Investment Options**: Familiarize yourself with the investment options available within your retirement plan. Learn about the risk and return profiles of different investment vehicles, such as stocks, bonds, and mutual funds. Consider your risk tolerance and investment goals when selecting your investment allocations.

3. **Reassess and Rebalance**: Regularly review your retirement plan investments to ensure they align with your long-term goals. Over time, market fluctuations may cause your portfolio to become unbalanced. Rebalancing involves adjusting your investments to maintain your desired asset allocation. Consider consulting with a financial advisor for personalized guidance.

4. **Take Advantage of Catch-Up Contributions**: If you're over 50 years old, take advantage of catch-up contributions. These additional contributions, allowed in certain retirement plans, allow older individuals to make larger contributions to their retirement accounts. Catch-up contributions can help accelerate your savings as you approach retirement age.

5. **Educate Yourself**: Take the time to educate yourself about retirement planning and investment strategies. Read books, attend seminars, or seek guidance from financial professionals. Building your knowledge will empower you to make informed decisions and optimize your retirement savings.

Insights from Renowned Experts:

1. **David Bach**: David Bach, author of "*Smart Women Finish Rich*" emphasizes the importance of taking advantage of employer-sponsored retirement plans. He advises individuals to contribute to these plans, such as 401(k) or 403(b) accounts, especially if employers offer matching contributions. Bach believes that participating in employer-sponsored retirement plans is a key component of building long-term wealth.

2. **Jane Bryant Quinn**: Jane Bryant Quinn, a renowned financial journalist and author, stresses the significance of employer-sponsored retirement plans in securing a comfortable retirement. She encourages individuals to contribute as much as possible to these plans, taking advantage of any employer matching contributions. Quinn believes that employer-sponsored retirement plans provide valuable tax advantages and should be maximized for retirement savings.

Book Examples:

1. "*The Automatic Millionaire*" by **David Bach**: David Bach's book highlights the benefits of employer-sponsored retirement plans as a vehicle for long-term wealth accumulation. He explains the advantages of contributing to these plans, such as tax benefits and potential employer matching contributions. Bach provides practical strategies for maximizing retirement plan contributions and leveraging them for financial success.

2. "*How to Make Your Money Last*" by **Jane Bryant Quinn**: In her book, Jane Bryant Quinn explores various retirement planning topics, including the importance of employer-sponsored retirement plans. She explains how these plans can provide individuals with a tax-advantaged way to save for retirement. Quinn offers insights into making the most of employer matches and optimizing retirement plan contributions.

Conclusion: Employer-sponsored retirement plans present an incredible opportunity for personal economic growth, finance management, and long-term wealth accumulation. By participating in these plans, you can take advantage of tax advantages, employer contributions, and the power of compounding. Make a conscious effort to enroll early, contribute consistently, and understand the investment options available to you. Educate yourself on retirement planning and seek professional guidance when needed. With careful planning and a proactive approach, you can secure your financial future and enjoy a fulfilling and prosperous life ahead.

11. Set specific financial goals and work towards achieving them.

By defining clear objectives and working towards them, you can build a solid foundation for your financial well-being. We will explore the importance of setting specific financial goals, how they contribute to personal growth, and practical strategies to achieve them.

Understanding the Power of Specific Financial Goals: Setting specific financial goals provides numerous benefits and serves as a roadmap to success:

1. **Clarity and Focus**: Specific financial goals give you a clear direction and purpose. They help you focus your efforts, enabling you to make deliberate choices and prioritize your financial decisions accordingly.

2. **Motivation and Accountability**: Having specific goals provides motivation and a sense of purpose. When you have a clear vision of what you want to achieve, it becomes easier to stay motivated and committed to your financial journey. Additionally, setting goals holds you accountable for your actions and encourages you to take consistent steps towards their attainment.

3. **Measurement of Progress**: Specific financial goals provide measurable milestones that allow you to track your progress. By monitoring your achievements, you can identify areas of improvement, celebrate your successes, and make necessary adjustments along the way.

Strategies for Setting and Achieving Specific Financial Goals:

1. **Define Your Goals**: Begin by identifying your financial aspirations. Do you want to save for a down payment on a house, pay off debt, start a business, or retire early? Be specific about what you want to achieve, including the amount of money involved and the timeline you aim to accomplish it in.

2. **Break Down Goals into Milestones**: Large financial goals can be overwhelming. Break them down into smaller, manageable milestones. For example, if your goal is to save $50,000 for a down payment in five years, aim to save $10,000 per year or roughly $833 per month. Breaking it down into smaller targets makes the goal more attainable and allows you to track progress more effectively.

3. **Make Goals SMART**: Use the SMART framework to make your goals **Specific, Measurable, Achievable, Relevant, and Time-bound**. For example, instead of setting a vague goal like "save more money," a SMART goal would be "save $5,000 over the next 12 months by reducing unnecessary expenses and increasing income."

4. **Create a Budget**: A budget is a powerful tool that helps you align your income and expenses with your financial goals. Track your income and expenses, identify areas where you can cut back, and allocate funds towards your goals. Utilize budgeting apps or spreadsheets to simplify the process and stay organized.

5. **Automate Savings**: Set up automatic transfers from your paycheck or checking account to a separate savings or investment account. This helps you save consistently without the temptation to spend the money elsewhere. Start with a small amount and gradually increase it as you become comfortable.

6. **Monitor and Adjust**: Regularly review your progress towards your financial goals. Make adjustments to your budget and savings plan if necessary. Life circumstances and priorities may change, so be flexible and adaptable in your approach.

7. **Seek Financial Education**: Educate yourself about personal finance and investment strategies. Books, online resources, and courses can provide valuable insights and guidance. Stay informed about financial news, market trends, and opportunities that align with your goals.

Insights from Renowned Experts:

1. **Brian Tracy**: Brian Tracy, a renowned motivational speaker and author of "*Goals!: How to Get Everything You Want—Faster Than You Ever Thought Possible*" emphasizes the importance of setting specific financial goals. He believes that having clear and measurable objectives is essential for achieving financial success. Tracy encourages individuals to identify their financial aspirations and create a plan of action to work towards them.

2. **T. Harv Eker**: T. Harv Eker, author of "*Secrets of the Millionaire Mind*" stresses the significance of setting specific financial goals. He encourages individuals to set both short-term and long-term goals to create a clear roadmap for financial achievement. Eker believes that setting specific goals helps individuals stay focused and motivated on their financial journey.

Other Book Examples:

1. "*The Millionaire Next Door*" by **Thomas J. Stanley** and **William D. Danko**: This book explores the habits and characteristics of millionaires. Stanley and Danko emphasize the importance of setting specific financial goals as a common trait among wealthy individuals. They highlight the correlation between goal-setting, disciplined saving, and long-term wealth accumulation.

2. "*The Compound Effect*" by **Darren Hardy**: Darren Hardy's book focuses on the power of small actions and consistent effort in achieving success. He emphasizes the significance of setting specific financial goals and working towards them incrementally. Hardy believes that setting clear goals helps individuals track progress, make necessary adjustments, and ultimately achieve financial success.

Conclusion: Setting specific financial goals is a key strategy for personal economic growth, finance management, and achieving success in both business and life. By clearly defining your objectives, breaking them down into actionable steps, and staying focused, you can make steady progress towards your financial aspirations. Remember to review and adjust your goals regularly, seek financial education, and celebrate your milestones along the way. With determination, discipline, and the power of specific financial goals, you can pave the way to a brighter and more prosperous future.

12. Avoid impulsive spending and practice mindful consumption.

By avoiding impulsive spending and adopting a more intentional approach to consumption, you can make informed financial decisions, prioritize your values, and achieve a healthier and more prosperous financial future. So we will explore the importance of avoiding impulsive spending, the benefits of mindful consumption, and practical strategies to incorporate it into your daily life.

Understanding the Impact of Impulsive Spending: Impulsive spending refers to making purchases on a whim without careful consideration of its value or alignment with your financial goals. It can have several negative consequences:

1. **Financial Stress**: Impulsive spending often leads to debt accumulation, financial instability, and increased stress. It hinders your ability to save, invest, and achieve long-term financial goals.

2. **Misaligned Priorities**: Without mindful consumption, you may prioritize immediate gratification over your true values and aspirations. This can result in regrettable purchases and a lack of fulfillment in the long run.

3. **Cluttered Living Spaces**: Impulsive spending often leads to accumulation of unnecessary possessions, cluttering your living spaces and making it harder to maintain an organized and peaceful environment.

Benefits of Mindful Consumption:

1. **Financial Empowerment**: Practicing mindful consumption gives you greater control over your finances. By consciously evaluating your spending choices, you can allocate your resources towards things that truly matter and align with your goals.

2. **Value-Based Decision Making**: Mindful consumption allows you to make choices based on your values and priorities. It encourages you to spend money on experiences, relationships, personal growth, and investments that contribute to your overall well-being and happiness.

3. **Reduced Environmental Impact**: Mindful consumption promotes sustainability and minimizes waste. By being more conscious of the products you buy and their environmental impact, you contribute to a healthier planet.

Strategies for Avoiding Impulsive Spending and Embracing Mindful Consumption:

1. **Define Your Financial Goals**: Establish clear financial goals that serve as a compass for your spending decisions. Whether it's saving for a down payment, starting a business, or achieving financial independence, having specific goals keeps you focused and less likely to engage in impulsive spending.

2. **Create a Budget**: Develop a budget that aligns with your financial goals. Track your income, categorize your expenses, and set realistic spending limits for different categories. Be mindful of your budget and refer to it before making any purchasing decisions.

3. **Practice the 24-Hour Rule**: Before making a non-essential purchase, implement the 24-hour rule. Give yourself time to reflect on the purchase and evaluate if it aligns with your values and priorities. This helps you avoid impulsive decisions and ensures your spending is intentional.

4. **Identify Triggers and Temptations**: Understand the triggers that lead to impulsive spending, such as emotional stress, social pressure, or online advertisements. Recognize these triggers and develop strategies to overcome them, such as finding healthier coping mechanisms or limiting exposure to tempting environments.

5. **Conduct Research and Comparison Shopping**: Before making significant purchases, research and compare prices, features, and reviews. This helps you make informed decisions and ensures you're getting the best value for your money.

6. **Practice Gratitude and Contentment**: Cultivate a mindset of gratitude and contentment with what you already have. Recognize and appreciate the abundance in your life, which reduces the desire for unnecessary purchases driven by a sense of lack or comparison to others.

7. **Seek Quality Over Quantity**: Focus on acquiring quality items that are durable, sustainable, and align with your long-term needs. Investing in high-quality products may require a higher upfront cost but can save you money in the long run.

8. **Engage in Alternative Forms of Entertainment**: Instead of mindlessly shopping or engaging in expensive activities, explore alternative forms of entertainment that are fulfilling and cost-effective. Engage in hobbies, spend time with loved ones, explore nature, or pursue personal development activities.

Conclusion: By avoiding impulsive spending and practicing mindful consumption, you can take control of your personal economic growth, finance, and overall management. Mindful consumption empowers you to make value-based decisions, reduce financial stress, and lead a more fulfilling life. Incorporate the strategies discussed, reflect on your spending habits, and embrace a more intentional approach to consumption. Remember, small changes in your daily choices can lead to significant long-term financial benefits and personal satisfaction.

Here are a few resources that may further assist you in understanding and adopting mindful consumption:

- "*Your Money or Your Life*" by **Vicki Robin** and **Joe Dominguez**
- "*The Minimalist Home*" by **Joshua Becker**
- "*The Joy of Less*" by **Francine Jay**
- "*The Art of Frugal Hedonism*" by **Annie Raser-Rowland** and **Adam Grubb**

13. Develop multiple streams of income to increase earning potential.

Relying solely on a single source of income can leave you vulnerable to economic uncertainties and limit your earning potential. We will explore the benefits of multiple streams of income, strategies to diversify your income sources, and practical steps to help you unlock your financial potential.

Understanding the Power of Multiple Streams of Income:

1. **Increased Financial Security**: Having multiple streams of income provides a safety net in case one source of income diminishes or becomes unstable. It reduces the risk of financial hardship and provides greater peace of mind, knowing that you have multiple sources to rely on.

2. **Enhanced Earning Potential**: Developing additional income streams allows you to tap into new revenue sources and maximize your earning potential. It opens up opportunities to generate income from various channels, increasing your overall financial capacity.

3. **Diversification**: Just as diversifying your investment portfolio reduces risk, diversifying your income sources spreads out your financial risk. If one stream of income experiences a downturn, the others can help mitigate the impact and maintain your financial stability.

Strategies for Developing Multiple Streams of Income:

1. **Identify Your Skills and Passions**: Start by assessing your skills, knowledge, and interests. Identify areas where you excel and have a passion for learning and growing. This self-reflection will help you determine the most viable income-generating opportunities that align with your strengths and personal interests.

2. **Explore Freelancing and Side Hustles**: Leverage your skills and expertise to offer freelance services or start a side business. Freelancing platforms and online marketplaces provide opportunities to showcase your talents and connect with potential clients. Whether it's writing, graphic design, consulting, or tutoring, explore avenues that allow you to monetize your skills on a flexible schedule.

3. **Create and Monetize Digital Assets**: In today's digital age, creating and monetizing digital assets can be a lucrative income stream. Consider developing a blog, YouTube channel, podcast, or online course to share your knowledge and expertise with a wider audience. Monetization options can include advertising, sponsorships, affiliate marketing, and selling digital products.

4. **Invest in Real Estate**: Real estate can be a powerful income-generating asset. Explore opportunities to invest in rental properties, either residential or commercial, and earn rental income. Alternatively, consider real estate crowdfunding platforms that allow you to invest in properties with smaller capital contributions.

5. **Start an E-commerce Business**: With the rise of e-commerce, starting an online business has become more accessible. Identify a niche market, source or create products, and establish an online store. Platforms like Shopify, Amazon and Etsy provide user-friendly tools to set up your business and reach customers worldwide.

6. **Invest in Dividend-Paying Stocks**: Invest in dividend-paying stocks to generate passive income. Dividend stocks distribute a portion of the company's profits to shareholders, providing regular income streams. Research and choose reliable companies with a history of consistent dividend payments and long-term growth potential.

7. **Leverage the Sharing Economy**: Take advantage of the sharing economy by monetizing your assets or skills. Rent out a spare room on platforms like Airbnb, offer your car for ride-sharing services like Uber or Lyft, or become a delivery driver for food delivery platforms. These options allow you to generate income using existing resources.

8. **Network and Collaborate**: Networking and collaboration can lead to new income opportunities. Attend industry events, join professional organizations, and connect with like-minded individuals. Collaborate on projects, partnerships, or joint ventures to leverage each other's strengths and expand your income potential.

Taking Action: To develop multiple streams of income, it's essential to take consistent action and maintain a long-term perspective. Start by identifying your desired income streams, create a plan, and set achievable goals. Allocate dedicated time and effort to each income stream, nurturing and expanding them over time.

Conclusion: Developing multiple streams of income is a powerful strategy for personal economic growth, financial security, and overall success in business and life. By diversifying your income sources, you increase your earning potential, reduce financial vulnerabilities, and open up opportunities for greater financial freedom. Embrace the strategies discussed in this article, adapt them to your unique circumstances, and take consistent action towards unlocking your full financial potential.

Here are a few resources that may further assist you in developing multiple streams of income:

- "*The Side Hustle: How to Turn Your Spare Time into $1,000 a Month or More*" by **Nick Loper**
- "*The 4-Hour Workweek*" by **Timothy Ferriss**
- "*The Millionaire Fastlane*" by **MJ DeMarco**
- "*Multiple Streams of Income*" by **Robert G. Allen**

14. Negotiate better deals on purchases and services.

Negotiation is a powerful skill that can positively impact your personal economic growth, financial success, and overall management. Whether you're making a major purchase, seeking favorable terms on a service, or aiming to secure better deals in various aspects of life, effective negotiation can make a significant difference. We will explore practical strategies and tips to help you become a better negotiator, allowing you to secure better deals and achieve your desired outcomes.

Understanding the Importance of Negotiation:

1. **Financial Savings**: Negotiating better deals allows you to save money on purchases and services. It enables you to obtain products or services at lower prices, secure discounts, or gain additional value for your money.

2. **Improved Financial Management**: By negotiating better deals, you optimize your financial resources and enhance your ability to manage your finances effectively. Negotiation helps you stretch your budget, increase your purchasing power, and make more informed financial decisions.

3. **Enhanced Confidence and Empowerment**: Developing negotiation skills boosts your confidence and empowers you in various areas of life. It enables you to advocate for your interests, assert your needs, and navigate challenging situations with assertiveness.

Strategies for Negotiating Better Deals:

1. **Research and Preparation**: Before entering into any negotiation, conduct thorough research to gather information about the product or service, its market value, and any available alternatives. This knowledge equips you with valuable insights and strengthens your negotiating position.

2. **Define Your Objectives**: Clearly identify your goals and desired outcomes before entering a negotiation. Establish your ideal terms, such as price, payment conditions, delivery, or additional services. Having a clear understanding of what you want helps you stay focused during the negotiation process.

3. **Understand the Other Party's Perspective**: Put yourself in the shoes of the other party and try to understand their motivations, needs, and constraints. This empathetic approach allows you to tailor your negotiation strategy and find mutually beneficial solutions.

4. **Effective Communication**: Develop strong communication skills to convey your points effectively during negotiations. Clearly articulate your needs, ask thoughtful questions, and actively listen to the other party. Effective communication fosters mutual understanding and builds rapport.

5. **Find Win-Win Solutions**: Aim for a win-win outcome where both parties feel satisfied with the negotiated terms. Look for creative solutions that address the interests of both parties and seek areas of compromise that can add value to the overall deal.

6. **Be Patient and Persistent**: Negotiation requires patience and persistence. Don't be afraid to ask for what you want and be prepared for potential

pushbacks. Maintain a positive attitude and keep the lines of communication open to find common ground.

7. **Leverage Alternatives and Competition**: Having alternatives strengthens your negotiating position. Research other options available in the market and use them as leverage during negotiations. Competition can create a sense of urgency and motivate the other party to offer more favorable terms.

8. **Timing and Flexibility**: Timing can play a crucial role in negotiations. Be aware of market conditions, sales cycles, or specific events that may influence the other party's willingness to negotiate. Remain flexible and open to exploring different possibilities.

Real-Life Examples and Tips for Successful Negotiation:

1. **Purchasing a Car**: Research the market value of the car you intend to buy, gather quotes from different dealerships, and be prepared to negotiate the price, financing terms, or additional features. Consider timing your purchase during end-of-month or end-of-year sales when dealers may be more motivated to offer discounts.

2. **Renting an Apartment**: Research rental prices in the area, gather information on comparable properties, and negotiate the monthly rent, lease terms, or inclusion of utilities. Show your reliability as a tenant and highlight any positive factors that may strengthen your negotiation position.

3. **Service Providers**: When dealing with service providers, such as contractors, freelancers, or consultants, seek multiple quotes, compare their offerings, and negotiate prices or project scope. Emphasize the value you bring as a client and explore long-term partnership opportunities.

4. **Salary Negotiation**: Before accepting a job offer or during performance reviews, gather market salary data, highlight your achievements, and negotiate for better compensation, benefits, or career development opportunities. Focus on the value you bring to the organization and the positive impact you can make.

Conclusion: Negotiation is a valuable skill that empowers you to secure better deals, save money, and navigate various aspects of business and life more effectively. By applying the strategies and tips outlined in this article, you can become a more skilled negotiator, unlocking opportunities for personal economic growth, financial success, and improved management. Remember, negotiation is a dynamic process that requires practice, adaptability, and a mindset of seeking mutual benefit. Embrace the art of negotiation, and you'll find yourself on the path to winning in business and life.

Here are a few resources that may further assist you in improving your negotiation skills:

- "*Getting to Yes: Negotiating Agreement Without Giving In*" by **Roger Fisher**, **William Ury**, and **Bruce Patton**
- "*Never Split the Difference: Negotiating As If Your Life Depended On It*" by **Chris Voss**
- "*Start with No: The Negotiating Tools That the Pros Don't Want You to Know*" by **Jim Camp**

15. Prioritize long-term value over short-term gains.

By focusing on sustainable growth, prudent financial decisions, and strategic management, you can build a solid foundation for personal economic growth, financial well-being, and overall success. So, we will explore the importance of prioritizing long-term value and provide practical tips to help you make informed decisions that will benefit you in the long run.

Understanding the Concept of Long-Term Value:

1. **Financial Stability and Security**: Prioritizing long-term value involves making decisions that contribute to your financial stability and security. It means setting aside short-term impulses in favor of strategies that will yield consistent growth, reduce financial risks, and protect your assets over time.
2. **Sustainable Growth**: Emphasizing long-term value means focusing on sustainable growth rather than chasing quick wins. It involves adopting a mindset of steady progress and investing in activities and opportunities that will yield long-lasting benefits.
3. **Risk Mitigation**: Prioritizing long-term value allows you to assess and mitigate potential risks. By considering the long-term consequences of your actions, you can make informed decisions that minimize risks and maximize opportunities.

Strategies for Prioritizing Long-Term Value:

1. **Goal Setting**: Start by defining your long-term goals in various areas of life, including financial, career, personal development, and relationships.

Theia Stewart

Member of PageTitans

I wanted to remind you of the **free gift** that you are welcome to download. There is free additional content.

To download your free copy, simply follow the link or scan the QR code. Please **don't forget to subscribe** to stay in touch with PageTitans.

http://pagetitans.com?page=0000G19

These goals will serve as your compass, guiding your decisions and actions towards long-term value.

2. **Financial Planning**: Develop a comprehensive financial plan that aligns with your long-term goals. This includes creating a budget, managing debt, saving for retirement, and investing wisely. Seek professional advice if needed to ensure your financial decisions support your long-term objectives.

3. **Investing for the Future**: Prioritize investments that offer long-term growth potential. Diversify your investment portfolio to spread risks and explore options such as stocks, bonds, real estate, and mutual funds. Consider your risk tolerance and consult with financial advisors for personalized guidance.

4. **Building Meaningful Relationships**: Cultivate genuine and lasting relationships with clients, colleagues, mentors, and friends. These connections provide support, opportunities for collaboration, and long-term benefits in both personal and professional spheres.

5. **Continuous Learning and Skill Development**: Invest in your personal and professional growth through continuous learning. Acquire new skills, stay updated with industry trends, and expand your knowledge base. Long-term value often stems from a commitment to self-improvement and adaptability.

6. **Ethical Decision-Making**: Prioritize ethical practices and integrity in your personal and professional dealings. Acting with honesty and transparency builds trust, enhances your reputation, and contributes to long-term success.

7. **Strategic Planning**: Develop a strategic mindset by considering the long-term implications of your decisions. Anticipate potential challenges, evaluate different scenarios, and make choices that align with your long-term vision.

8. **Embrace Delayed Gratification**: Learn to delay instant gratification and make choices that contribute to long-term value. This may involve saving for major purchases, resisting impulsive buying decisions, or investing time and effort in building a solid foundation for future success.

Real-Life Examples and Benefits of Prioritizing Long-Term Value:

1. **Business Strategy**: Successful companies prioritize long-term value by investing in research and development, employee training, and sustainable

practices. This approach leads to innovation, customer loyalty, and increased market share.

2. **Personal Finance**: By saving and investing for the long term, you can enjoy financial security, retire comfortably, and leave a legacy for future generations. Compound interest and long-term investment returns can significantly boost your wealth over time.

3. **Career Growth**: Prioritizing long-term value in your career involves setting goals, acquiring new skills, and building a strong professional network. This approach opens doors to better job opportunities, promotions, and increased job satisfaction.

4. **Personal Development**: Investing time and effort in personal development activities, such as learning new skills, adopting healthy habits, and nurturing relationships, leads to personal fulfillment, improved well-being, and greater resilience in facing life's challenges.

Conclusion: Prioritizing long-term value is a powerful approach to achieving success in business and life. By focusing on sustainable growth, prudent financial decisions, and strategic management, you can build a solid foundation for personal economic growth, financial well-being, and overall fulfillment. Embrace the mindset of delayed gratification, make informed choices aligned with your long-term goals, and enjoy the benefits of a life well-lived. Remember, success is not just about the present moment; it's about creating a lasting impact that extends far into the future.

Here are a few recommended resources for further reading on personal finance, management, and long-term value:

- "*The Millionaire Next Door: The Surprising Secrets of America's Wealthy*" by **Thomas J. Stanley** and **William D. Danko**
- "*Essentialism: The Disciplined Pursuit of Less*" by **Greg McKeown**
- "*The Lean Startup: How Today's Entrepreneurs Use Continuous Innovation to Create Radically Successful Businesses*" by **Eric Ries**

16. Invest in your education and develop new skills for career growth.

By continuously learning and acquiring new skills, you expand your knowledge base, enhance your marketability, and position yourself for advancement in your chosen field. We will explore the importance of investing in education and skill development, and provide practical tips to help you achieve personal and professional growth.

The Benefits of Education and Skill Development:

1. **Career Advancement**: Acquiring new knowledge and skills opens doors to career advancement opportunities. Employers value employees who demonstrate a commitment to continuous learning and are equipped with the latest industry knowledge and expertise.

2. **Increased Earning Potential**: Higher education and specialized skills often lead to higher earning potential. The investment you make in your education and skill development can result in better job prospects, promotions, and increased income over the course of your career.

3. **Adaptability in a Changing Job Market**: The job market is constantly evolving, and new technologies and trends can disrupt traditional career paths. By investing in education and skill development, you remain agile and adaptable, equipped to navigate changes and embrace new opportunities.

4. **Personal Growth and Confidence**: Education and skill development contribute to personal growth, self-confidence, and a sense of accomplishment. Acquiring new knowledge and mastering new skills expands your horizons, broadens your perspective, and boosts your self-esteem.

Strategies for Investing in Education and Skill Development:

1. **Set Clear Goals**: Define your career goals and identify the knowledge and skills required to achieve them. This clarity will guide your educational pursuits and help you make informed decisions about the areas in which you should invest your time and resources.

2. **Pursue Higher Education**: Consider pursuing formal education through universities, colleges, or online platforms. Evaluate degree programs, certifications, or specialized courses that align with your career aspirations. Research institutions known for their quality programs and alumni success.

3. **Continuous Learning**: Embrace a lifelong learning mindset. Seek out opportunities to learn and grow, such as attending seminars, workshops, and conferences. Leverage online learning platforms that offer a wide range of courses on various subjects, including business, technology, leadership, and finance.

4. **Develop Transferable Skills**: Identify skills that are in high demand across industries, such as critical thinking, problem-solving, communication, and leadership. Invest time in developing these transferable skills, as they will enhance your marketability and adaptability in different professional settings.

5. **Seek Mentors and Coaches**: Connect with mentors and coaches who can provide guidance, support, and insights based on their experience and expertise. They can offer valuable advice on career development, skill-building strategies, and navigating professional challenges.

6. **Network and Collaborate**: Engage in networking activities within your industry or area of interest. Join professional organizations, attend industry events, and connect with like-minded professionals. Collaboration and networking provide opportunities to learn from others, share knowledge, and stay updated on industry trends.

7. **Embrace Online Resources**: Take advantage of online resources, such as webinars, podcasts, and e-books, that offer valuable insights from industry experts. Online communities and forums also provide platforms for knowledge sharing and collaboration with peers.

8. **Apply Learning to Real-Life Situations**: Actively seek opportunities to apply the knowledge and skills you acquire. Look for projects, internships, or volunteer work that allow you to practice and refine your abilities in real-world settings.

Real-Life Examples of Investing in Education and Skill Development:

1. **Mark Zuckerberg**: The co-founder of Facebook prioritized continuous learning by setting a personal goal to read a new book every two weeks. This commitment to self-education has contributed to his success as a technology entrepreneur and business leader.

2. **Sheryl Sandberg**: The Chief Operating Officer of Facebook, Sheryl Sandberg, emphasized the importance of ongoing skill development in her book "*Lean In*" She encourages individuals to take risks, seek challenges, and continually develop their skills to advance their careers.

Conclusion: Investing in your education and skill development is a powerful strategy for personal economic growth, financial prosperity, and career advancement. By embracing a lifelong learning mindset, setting clear goals, and actively seeking opportunities to acquire new knowledge and skills, you position yourself for success in business and in life. Remember, the journey of personal growth and development is ongoing, so commit to investing in yourself and enjoy the rewards of a fulfilling and prosperous future.

Here are some recommended resources for further reading on personal finance, skill development, and lifelong learning:

- "*Mindset: The New Psychology of Success*" by **Carol S. Dweck**
- "*The Personal MBA: Master the Art of Business*" by **Josh Kaufman**
- "*Deep Work: Rules for Focused Success in a Distracted World*" by **Cal Newport**

17. Consider real estate investment opportunities.

One avenue that has consistently shown potential for wealth creation is real estate investment. We will delve into the world of real estate investment, discussing its benefits, strategies, and key considerations. Whether you're a seasoned investor or just starting out, understanding real estate investment can help you build long-term financial stability and success.

The Benefits of Real Estate Investment:

1. **Potential for Appreciation**: Real estate has the potential to appreciate in value over time. Historically, properties tend to increase in value, allowing investors to generate significant returns on their initial investment.

2. **Cash Flow Generation**: Rental properties can provide a consistent stream of passive income. By investing in properties that generate positive cash flow, you can create an additional income source to supplement your primary earnings.

3. **Diversification**: Real estate investment offers diversification benefits to your investment portfolio. It is an asset class that behaves differently from stocks, bonds, or mutual funds, which can help reduce overall investment risk.

4. **Tax Advantages**: Real estate investment offers various tax benefits, including deductions for mortgage interest, property taxes, depreciation, and operating expenses. These tax advantages can significantly reduce your tax liability and increase your net income.

5. **Hedge against Inflation**: Real estate investments have the potential to provide a hedge against inflation. As rental income and property values

increase with inflation, your investment can retain its value and potentially outpace inflation rates.

Strategies for Real Estate Investment:

1. **Define Your Investment Goals**: Determine your financial objectives and align them with your real estate investment strategy. Are you seeking long-term appreciation, cash flow, or a combination of both? Clarifying your goals will help you make informed decisions throughout the investment process.

2. **Research and Market Analysis**: Conduct thorough research on the real estate market you wish to invest in. Analyze local market trends, property values, rental demand, and economic indicators to identify areas with growth potential and favorable investment conditions.

3. **Financial Planning and Budgeting**: Create a comprehensive financial plan and set a budget for your real estate investment. Consider factors such as down payment, financing options, closing costs, ongoing maintenance expenses, property management fees, and potential vacancy periods.

4. **Investment Property Analysis**: Perform due diligence on potential investment properties. Evaluate factors such as location, property condition, rental potential, and potential renovation costs. Conduct a comparative market analysis to determine if the property is priced competitively.

5. **Financing Options**: Explore different financing options, including mortgages, private lenders, or partnerships. Compare interest rates, loan terms, and down payment requirements to find the most suitable financing option for your investment.

6. **Property Management**: Determine whether you will manage the property yourself or hire a professional property management company. Property managers can handle tenant screening, rent collection, maintenance, and other day-to-day responsibilities, allowing you to focus on your core investment strategy.

7. **Risk Management**: Assess and mitigate potential risks associated with real estate investment. Consider factors such as market volatility, interest rate fluctuations, tenant turnover, and unforeseen repairs. Adequate risk management strategies will help protect your investment and minimize potential losses.

8. **Continuous Learning**: Stay informed about real estate investment trends, regulations, and best practices. Attend seminars, workshops, and networking events to learn from experienced investors and industry professionals. Continuous learning will sharpen your investment skills and keep you up to date with changing market dynamics.

Book Examples:

1. "*The Book on Rental Property Investing*" by **Brandon Turner**: This book provides a comprehensive guide to investing in rental properties. It covers various aspects of real estate investing, including property selection, financing, property management, and building wealth through rental income. Brandon Turner shares his personal experiences and provides practical strategies for successful real estate investing.

2. "*The Millionaire Real Estate Investor*" by **Gary Keller**, **Dave Jenks**, and **Jay Papasan**: In this book, the authors present a roadmap for achieving financial success through real estate investing. They share insights from interviews with successful real estate investors and provide valuable tips on identifying profitable investment opportunities, managing properties, and creating wealth through real estate.

3. "*Rich Dad, Poor Dad*" by **Robert Kiyosaki**: Although not solely focused on real estate investing, this influential book by Robert Kiyosaki highlights the importance of investing in income-generating assets, including real estate. Kiyosaki shares his perspective on financial literacy, wealth-building, and the advantages of investing in tangible assets like real estate to generate passive income and achieve financial independence.

4. "*The Book on Investing in Real Estate with No (and Low) Money Down*" by **Brandon Turner** and **David Greene**: This book addresses the common misconception that real estate investing requires significant upfront capital. The authors explore various creative financing strategies, such as partnerships, seller financing, and leveraging other people's money, to help readers get started in real estate investing with minimal or no money down.

5. "*The ABCs of Real Estate Investing*" by **Ken McElroy**: Ken McElroy, a real estate investor and author, shares his insights on successful real estate investing in this book. He covers topics such as market analysis, property valuation, financing options, property management, and creating a sustainable real estate portfolio. McElroy's book provides practical advice for both beginner and experienced real estate investors.

Real-Life Examples of Successful Real Estate Investors:

1. **Barbara Corcoran**: The renowned real estate entrepreneur and investor, Barbara Corcoran, built a successful real estate empire by identifying market

2. **Donald Bren**: Donald Bren is an American real estate developer and businessman who is the chairman and owner of the Irvine Company, a real estate development company based in California. He is known for his strategic investments in commercial and residential properties, particularly in the Southern California region. With a keen eye for market trends and urban planning, Bren has become one of the wealthiest real estate investors in the United States.

3. **Sam Zell**: Sam Zell is a prominent real estate investor and businessman known for his savvy investments and contrarian approach. He founded Equity Group Investments, a private investment firm, and has a track record of successful real estate acquisitions, including office buildings, apartment complexes, and shopping centers. Zell's ability to identify undervalued properties and turn them into profitable ventures has earned him a reputation as a shrewd investor.

4. **Stephen Ross**: Stephen Ross is the chairman and founder of Related Companies, a real estate development firm known for its high-profile projects such as the Hudson Yards in New York City. Ross has been involved in various types of real estate investments, ranging from residential and commercial properties to sports and entertainment venues. His ability to envision and execute large-scale developments has made him a key player in the real estate industry.

5. **Zhang Xin**: Zhang Xin is a Chinese businesswoman and co-founder of SOHO China, a leading commercial property developer. She is known for her astute investments in the Chinese real estate market, particularly in high-demand areas such as Beijing and Shanghai. Zhang Xin's entrepreneurial spirit and ability to adapt to changing market conditions have contributed to her success in the real estate industry.

6. **Jonathan Gray**: Jonathan Gray is the President and Chief Operating Officer of Blackstone Group, one of the world's largest investment firms. Gray oversees the firm's real estate division, which has been involved in significant real estate investments globally. His expertise in identifying attractive investment opportunities and executing complex transactions has positioned Blackstone as a major player in the real estate investment landscape.

These real-life examples illustrate the diverse paths and strategies employed by successful real estate investors. While each investor has their unique approach, common themes include a deep understanding of the market, the ability to identify value and growth potential, and a willingness to take calculated risks. Learning from the experiences of these successful investors can provide valuable insights and inspiration for your own real estate investment journey.

18. Regularly review and optimize your investment portfolio.

A well-structured and optimized portfolio can help you achieve your financial goals and build long-term wealth. We will explore the importance of regularly reviewing and optimizing your investment portfolio, providing practical tips and insights to help you make informed decisions along the way.

The Power of Regular Portfolio Reviews:

1. **Assessing Performance**: Regular portfolio reviews allow you to evaluate the performance of your investments. By analyzing the returns, you can identify areas of strength and weakness, enabling you to make adjustments to enhance your portfolio's performance.

2. **Identifying Diversification Gaps**: Reviewing your portfolio helps you assess the diversification of your investments. Diversification is key to managing risk and optimizing returns. By identifying any concentration or imbalance in your asset allocation, you can make necessary adjustments to achieve a well-diversified portfolio.

3. **Aligning with Financial Goals**: Life circumstances and financial goals evolve over time. Regular portfolio reviews enable you to realign your investments with your changing objectives. Whether you're saving for retirement, a down payment on a house, or funding your children's education, reviewing your portfolio ensures it remains in line with your aspirations.

4. **Capitalizing on Opportunities**: Financial markets are dynamic, presenting new investment opportunities regularly. By reviewing your portfolio, you can identify emerging trends, sectors, or asset classes that may provide attractive prospects for growth. This flexibility allows you to seize potential opportunities to maximize returns.

Tips for Optimizing Your Investment Portfolio:

1. **Define Your Investment Strategy**: Clearly articulate your investment objectives, risk tolerance, and time horizon. This foundation will guide your decision-making process when reviewing and optimizing your portfolio.

2. **Conduct Regular Reviews**: Set a schedule to review your portfolio periodically. Depending on your investment horizon and goals, quarterly or annual reviews are generally recommended. This regular cadence ensures you stay proactive and responsive to market changes.

3. **Assess Asset Allocation**: Evaluate the allocation of your investments across different asset classes, such as stocks, bonds, real estate, and commodities. Adjust your allocations based on market conditions, economic trends, and your risk appetite to optimize your portfolio's performance.

4. **Rebalance Your Portfolio**: Rebalancing involves adjusting the weightings of your investments to maintain the desired asset allocation. When certain investments outperform others, they may become overrepresented in your portfolio. Rebalancing allows you to sell overperforming assets and allocate funds to underperforming or undervalued assets.

5. **Consider Tax Efficiency**: Tax implications play a crucial role in investment outcomes. Optimize your portfolio for tax efficiency by utilizing tax-advantaged accounts, such as individual retirement accounts (IRAs) or 401(k) plans. Additionally, evaluate tax-efficient investment strategies, such as holding tax-efficient funds or employing tax-loss harvesting techniques.

6. **Stay Informed**: Keep yourself updated on market trends, economic indicators, and industry news. Read financial publications, follow reputable investment websites, and leverage technology tools that provide real-time market insights. Staying informed allows you to make informed decisions when reviewing and optimizing your portfolio.

7. **Seek Professional Advice**: If you feel overwhelmed or lack expertise in portfolio management, consider consulting a financial advisor. A trusted advisor can provide personalized guidance, assess your risk profile, and help optimize your investment portfolio based on your specific goals and circumstances.

Renowned Experts:

1. **Warren Buffett**: Warren Buffett, widely regarded as one of the most successful investors in the world, emphasizes the importance of regularly reviewing and optimizing your investment portfolio. He advises investors to focus on long-term value and to make adjustments to their portfolio based on changes in market conditions and individual investment performance.

2. **Ray Dalio**: Ray Dalio, the founder of Bridgewater Associates, emphasizes the need for diversification and constant review of investment portfolios. He advocates for a systematic approach to investing and suggests regularly reassessing investment allocations to ensure they align with one's financial goals and risk tolerance.

3. **Peter Lynch**: Peter Lynch, a legendary investor and former manager of the Fidelity Magellan Fund, encourages investors to stay actively involved in managing their portfolios. He advises investors to regularly review their holdings, assess their performance, and make necessary adjustments to optimize returns.

Book Examples:

1. "*The Intelligent Investor*" by **Benjamin Graham**: Although primarily focused on value investing, this book by Benjamin Graham emphasizes the importance of regularly reviewing and optimizing investment portfolios. Graham highlights the need for a disciplined approach to investing, which includes periodically assessing the performance of individual stocks and making adjustments based on market conditions and investment objectives.

2. "*A Random Walk Down Wall Street*" by **Burton G. Malkiel**: This classic investment book highlights the importance of regularly reviewing and rebalancing investment portfolios. Malkiel emphasizes the concept of efficient market hypothesis and suggests that investors should periodically reassess their portfolio allocations to maintain a balance between risk and return.

3. "*Common Stocks and Uncommon Profits*" by **Philip Fisher**: Philip Fisher, a renowned investor, discusses the importance of continuously reviewing and evaluating investment holdings. He emphasizes the need for thorough research and ongoing monitoring of company fundamentals to ensure the investments align with one's investment objectives and to make necessary adjustments when required.

4. "*The Four Pillars of Investing*" by **William Bernstein**: In this book, William Bernstein emphasizes the importance of regularly reviewing and optimizing investment portfolios. He discusses the four key principles of successful investing and provides practical advice on how to assess portfolio performance, rebalance asset allocations, and make informed decisions based on changing market conditions.

Conclusion: Regularly reviewing and optimizing your investment portfolio is a vital aspect of personal economic growth, finance, and management. It allows you to assess performance, diversify your holdings, align with financial goals, and capitalize on opportunities. By following the tips provided and staying informed, you can make well-informed decisions that maximize the potential of your investment portfolio. Remember, investing is a dynamic process, and adapting to changing market conditions is key to achieving long-term financial success.

19. Start a side business or freelancing gig for additional income.

One effective strategy is starting a side business or freelancing gig to generate additional income. We will explore the benefits of embarking on such ventures and provide practical advice on how to get started.

The Power of a Side Business or Freelancing Gig:

1. **Supplementing Income**: A side business or freelancing gig offers the opportunity to augment your primary income stream. By diversifying your sources of revenue, you can increase your earning potential, improve financial resilience, and achieve your goals more rapidly.

2. **Exploring Passion Projects**: Starting a side business allows you to pursue your passion and turn it into a profitable endeavor. Whether it's offering a service, creating a product, or monetizing a hobby, a side business enables you to follow your interests and potentially generate income doing what you love.

3. **Developing Entrepreneurial Skills**: Launching and managing a side business or freelancing gig provides a valuable learning experience. You gain hands-on knowledge in areas such as marketing, finance, customer service, and operations. These skills can enhance your overall professional profile and open doors to new opportunities.

4. **Broadening Networks**: Building a side business or freelancing gig introduces you to a diverse network of clients, customers, and industry professionals. Networking can lead to collaborations, partnerships, and future business prospects, expanding your professional connections and creating further income-generating possibilities.

Getting Started with a Side Business or Freelancing Gig:

1. **Identify Your Strengths and Passions**: Begin by identifying your skills, expertise, and interests. What unique value can you offer? Consider your hobbies, professional experience, and knowledge areas that others may find valuable.

2. **Conduct Market Research**: Evaluate the demand and competition in your chosen field. Identify your target audience, understand their needs, and analyze existing businesses or freelancers offering similar services or products. Differentiating yourself and finding a niche can enhance your chances of success.

3. **Define Your Business Model**: Determine the nature of your side business or freelancing gig. Will it involve providing services, selling products, or a combination? Clarify your pricing strategy, revenue streams, and how you plan to reach your target market.

4. **Create a Business Plan**: Develop a clear and concise business plan that outlines your objectives, target market, marketing strategies, financial projections, and growth plans. A business plan serves as a roadmap, guiding your actions and helping you stay focused on your goals.

5. **Establish a Strong Online Presence**: In today's digital age, having an online presence is crucial for reaching a wider audience. Create a professional website or online portfolio that showcases your services or products. Utilize social media platforms to promote your offerings, engage with potential clients, and build a community around your brand.

6. **Cultivate Relationships and Leverage Existing Networks**: Tap into your existing personal and professional networks to spread the word about your side business or freelancing gig. Attend industry events, join relevant online communities, and actively engage with potential clients or collaborators. Networking is a powerful tool for generating leads and expanding your reach.

7. **Deliver Exceptional Value and Customer Service**: Strive to exceed customer expectations by delivering high-quality products or services.

Word-of-mouth recommendations are invaluable, and satisfied customers can become repeat clients or refer you to others.

Renowned Experts:

1. **Gary Vaynerchuk**: Gary Vaynerchuk, a successful entrepreneur and author, often emphasizes the value of starting a side business or pursuing freelancing gigs. He encourages individuals to leverage their skills and passions to generate additional income and diversify their revenue streams.

2. **Brian Chesky and Joe Gebbia (Airbnb)**. Brian Chesky and Joe Gebbia, the founders of Airbnb, started their business as a side project to earn additional income. They rented out air mattresses in their apartment during a conference when hotels were scarce. This small venture eventually grew into a global phenomenon, revolutionizing the hospitality industry. Chesky and Gebbia's story exemplifies the transformative power of a side business that starts with a simple idea and evolves into a multi-billion-dollar enterprise.

3. **Chris Guillebeau**: Chris Guillebeau, known for his book "*Side Hustle: From Idea to Income in 27 Days*" encourages people to start side businesses to increase their income and create financial security. He provides practical advice on identifying profitable side business ideas and turning them into successful ventures.

4. **Robert Kiyosaki**: Robert Kiyosaki, the author of "*Rich Dad Poor Dad*" advocates for the importance of entrepreneurship and creating multiple streams of income. He believes that starting a side business or freelancing gig can provide financial independence and open doors to greater opportunities.

Other Book Examples:

1. "*The $100 Startup*" by **Chris Guillebeau**: In this book, Chris Guillebeau shares inspiring stories of individuals who started successful businesses with minimal investment. He provides practical guidance on finding profitable business ideas, validating them, and launching them as side businesses for additional income.

2. "*The 4-Hour Workweek*" by **Timothy Ferriss**: While not solely focused on side businesses, this book by Timothy Ferriss explores ways to achieve financial freedom and create a flexible lifestyle. Ferriss suggests methods for automating and outsourcing work to free up time for pursuing side businesses or other income-generating activities.

3. "*The Lean Startup*" by **Eric Ries**: Although primarily focused on startups, this book offers valuable insights for individuals looking to start a side business. Eric Ries introduces the concept of a minimum viable product (MVP) and provides guidance on testing ideas, iterating, and building a successful business with limited resources.

Conclusion: Starting a side business or freelancing gig can be a game-changer for personal economic growth, finance, and management. It offers the opportunity to supplement income, explore passion projects, develop entrepreneurial skills, and expand professional networks. By following the steps outlined and drawing inspiration from real-life success stories like Airbnb, you can embark on your own journey towards financial empowerment and fulfillment. Remember, the key to success lies in identifying your strengths, researching the market, and delivering exceptional value to your customers. Start today, and unlock your potential for additional income and personal growth.

20. Protect yourself and your assets through insurance.

Insurance plays a vital role in providing a safety net, offering financial protection and peace of mind. We will explore the importance of insurance, different types of coverage, and practical tips to ensure you have the necessary protection in place.

The Importance of Insurance:

1. **Financial Security**: Insurance serves as a safety net, providing financial protection against risks and uncertainties. It acts as a shield that helps mitigate the financial impact of unfortunate events such as accidents, illnesses, natural disasters, and property damage.

2. **Asset Protection**: Insurance safeguards your assets, including your home, vehicle, business, and personal belongings. Adequate coverage ensures that you can recover from unexpected losses or damages without incurring significant financial setbacks.

3. **Health and Well-being**: Health insurance is crucial for protecting your well-being and managing medical expenses. It provides access to quality healthcare services and can alleviate the financial burden of unexpected medical emergencies or ongoing treatments.

4. **Legal Obligations**: Certain types of insurance, such as auto insurance, are required by law. Meeting these obligations ensures compliance with legal

requirements and protects you from potential liabilities in case of accidents or damages caused by your vehicle.

Types of Insurance Coverage:

1. **Health Insurance**: Health insurance provides coverage for medical expenses, including doctor visits, hospital stays, surgeries, medications, and preventive care. It is essential to choose a plan that aligns with your healthcare needs and offers adequate coverage for you and your family.

2. **Property Insurance**: Property insurance protects your home, rental property, or business premises against damages caused by fire, theft, natural disasters, or other covered perils. It typically covers the physical structure and contents, providing financial compensation for repairs, replacement, or rebuilding.

3. **Auto Insurance**: Auto insurance provides coverage for damages or injuries caused by accidents involving your vehicle. It typically includes liability coverage (to protect against damages to others), collision coverage (for damages to your vehicle), and comprehensive coverage (for non-collision-related damages).

4. **Life Insurance**: Life insurance provides financial protection to your loved ones in the event of your death. It can help cover funeral expenses, outstanding debts, mortgages, and provide ongoing financial support for your family.

5. **Disability Insurance**: Disability insurance replaces a portion of your income if you become disabled and are unable to work. It provides a vital source of income during periods of disability when you may be unable to earn a living.

Tips for Ensuring Adequate Insurance Coverage:

1. **Assess Your Needs**: Evaluate your personal and financial circumstances to determine the types and amount of insurance coverage you require. Consider factors such as your age, health, dependents, assets, and potential risks.

2. **Research and Compare Policies**: Shop around and obtain quotes from multiple insurance providers to compare coverage options, premiums, deductibles, and policy terms. Carefully review policy documents to understand the coverage details, exclusions, and limitations.

3. **Consult with an Insurance Professional**: Seeking guidance from an insurance agent or broker can help you navigate the complexities of

insurance and find the best coverage options for your specific needs. They can provide expert advice and help tailor policies to your requirements.

4. **Review and Update Regularly**: Regularly review your insurance policies to ensure they align with your current circumstances and needs. Major life events such as marriage, having children, buying a new home, or starting a business may warrant adjustments to your coverage.

5. **Bundle Policies for Savings**: Consider bundling multiple insurance policies with the same provider to potentially save on premiums. Many insurance companies offer discounts when you combine auto, home, and other policies.

6. **Maintain Good Records**: Keep organized records of your insurance policies, premium payments, and any communication with your insurance provider. This will facilitate the claims process and ensure a smooth experience during times of need.

7. **Understand Policy Exclusions and Limitations**: Familiarize yourself with the exclusions and limitations of your insurance policies to avoid surprises when filing a claim. Be aware of any specific conditions or actions that may void your coverage.

Renowned Experts:

1. **Suze Orman**: Suze Orman, a renowned personal finance expert and author, stresses the importance of insurance in protecting oneself and assets. She emphasizes the need for adequate health insurance, life insurance, disability insurance, and homeowners/renters insurance to safeguard against unexpected events and financial hardships.

2. **Dave Ramsey**: Dave Ramsey, a well-known financial author and radio host, advises individuals to prioritize insurance as part of their overall financial plan. He emphasizes the significance of having adequate coverage for health, home, auto, and life insurance to mitigate risks and protect against financial setbacks.

3. **Tony Robbins**: Tony Robbins, a motivational speaker and life coach, highlights the role of insurance in providing financial security and peace of mind. He emphasizes the need to assess one's insurance needs and obtain appropriate coverage to protect against unforeseen circumstances that could have a significant impact on one's financial well-being.

Book Examples:

1. "*The Money Book for the Young, Fabulous & Broke*" by **Suze Orman**: In this book, Suze Orman discusses the importance of insurance as part of a comprehensive financial plan. She provides guidance on selecting the right insurance policies, understanding coverage options, and ensuring adequate protection for oneself and assets.

2. "*The Total Money Makeover*" by **Dave Ramsey**: While primarily focused on overall financial transformation, this book by Dave Ramsey emphasizes the significance of insurance in securing one's financial future. Ramsey provides insights on insurance essentials and guides readers on making informed decisions to protect their assets and loved ones.

3. "*Unshakeable*" by **Tony Robbins**: In this book, Tony Robbins explores strategies for achieving financial freedom and stability. He addresses the importance of insurance as a critical component of financial protection and resilience. Robbins shares insights on evaluating insurance needs, understanding policy terms, and securing appropriate coverage.

Conclusion: Insurance is a critical component of personal economic growth, finance, and management. It provides a safety net that safeguards your financial well-being, protects your assets, and offers peace of mind. By understanding your insurance needs, researching and comparing policies, and staying proactive in reviewing and updating your coverage, you can ensure that you are adequately protected against unexpected events. Remember, insurance is an investment in your future and a crucial step towards securing your financial stability and peace of mind.

21. Maximize tax-efficient savings and investment accounts.

These kind of accounts offer unique advantages that can help you save money on taxes, boost your investment returns, and accelerate your path to financial success. We will explore different tax-efficient accounts, strategies to maximize their benefits, and practical tips to optimize your savings and investments.

Understanding Tax-Efficient Accounts:

1. **Individual Retirement Accounts (IRAs)**: IRAs are popular retirement savings vehicles that offer tax advantages. Traditional IRAs allow you to contribute pre-tax dollars, reducing your current taxable income, while

Roth IRAs provide tax-free withdrawals in retirement. Both types of IRAs offer potential tax-deferred growth, allowing your investments to grow without being subject to annual taxes.

2. **401(k) and Employer-Sponsored Retirement Plans**: If your employer offers a 401(k) or similar retirement plan, take advantage of it. These plans allow you to contribute a portion of your pre-tax income, reducing your current tax liability. Some employers may even match a percentage of your contributions, providing an additional boost to your retirement savings.

3. **Health Savings Accounts (HSAs)**: HSAs are available to individuals with high-deductible health insurance plans. Contributions to an HSA are tax-deductible, and withdrawals are tax-free when used for qualified medical expenses. HSAs offer a triple tax advantage, making them a powerful tool for saving and investing for healthcare costs in retirement.

4. **529 College Savings Plans**: If you have children or plan to pursue higher education yourself, consider a 529 college savings plan. These plans allow you to contribute after-tax dollars, but the earnings grow tax-free, and withdrawals are tax-free when used for qualified education expenses. Some states also offer tax deductions or credits for contributions to 529 plans.

Maximizing Tax-Efficient Savings and Investments:

1. **Contribute the Maximum**: Aim to contribute the maximum allowed amount to your tax-efficient accounts each year. Take advantage of employer matching contributions in retirement plans, as this is essentially free money that can significantly boost your savings.

2. **Start Early**: The power of compounding is amplified when you start saving and investing early. The longer your money has to grow tax-free or tax-deferred, the greater the potential returns. Make saving for retirement and other long-term goals a priority from the beginning.

3. **Diversify Your Investments**: Spread your investments across different asset classes, such as stocks, bonds, and real estate, to minimize risk and maximize potential returns. Consider tax-efficient investment strategies, such as holding tax-efficient funds in taxable accounts and tax-inefficient investments in tax-advantaged accounts.

4. **Harvest Tax Losses**: Tax-loss harvesting involves selling investments that have experienced losses to offset capital gains and reduce your tax liability. This strategy can be particularly beneficial in taxable investment accounts, where you can use the losses to offset gains and potentially reduce your overall tax bill.

5. **Rebalance Regularly**: Periodically review and rebalance your investment portfolio to maintain your desired asset allocation. Rebalancing involves selling investments that have performed well and buying more of those that have underperformed. This practice helps you maintain a balanced and tax-efficient portfolio.

6. **Consider Roth Conversions**: If you have a traditional IRA or 401(k) and anticipate being in a lower tax bracket in certain years, consider converting some of your traditional retirement accounts to a Roth IRA. This conversion allows you to pay taxes now at a lower rate and enjoy tax-free withdrawals in retirement.

7. **Seek Professional Guidance**: Tax laws and investment strategies can be complex. Consider consulting a financial advisor or tax professional who can help you navigate the intricacies of tax-efficient savings and investment accounts. They can provide personalized advice based on your unique financial situation and goals.

Insights from Renowned Experts:

1. **Barbara Weltman**: Barbara Weltman, a renowned tax expert and author, emphasizes the importance of maximizing tax-efficient savings and investment accounts. She advises individuals to take advantage of tax-advantaged accounts, such as IRAs (Individual Retirement Accounts) and 401(k)s, to minimize their tax liability and maximize their savings. Weltman believes that utilizing these accounts can help individuals grow their wealth more efficiently.

2. **Eric Tyson**: Eric Tyson, author of *"Personal Finance for Dummies"* stresses the significance of maximizing tax-efficient savings and investment accounts. He encourages individuals to contribute the maximum allowed amounts to retirement accounts like IRAs and 401(k)s. Tyson explains the potential tax benefits of these accounts and how they can accelerate wealth accumulation over time.

Book Examples:

1. *"The Bogleheads' Guide to Retirement Planning"* by **Taylor Larimore**, **Mel Lindauer**, and **Richard A. Ferri**: This book, written by a group of financial experts, provides comprehensive guidance on retirement planning. The authors emphasize the importance of maximizing tax-efficient savings and investment accounts, such as IRAs and 401(k)s. They offer insights into strategies for optimizing contributions and leveraging tax advantages.

2. *"The Little Book of Common Sense Investing"* by **John C. Bogle**: John C. Bogle, the founder of Vanguard Group, explores the benefits of low-cost index fund investing. While the book primarily focuses on investment strategies, Bogle highlights the significance of tax-efficient accounts, such as IRAs and 401(k)s, in maximizing investment returns and minimizing taxes.

Conclusion: Maximizing tax-efficient savings and investment accounts is a key strategy for personal economic growth, finance, and management. By taking advantage of the tax benefits offered by accounts like IRAs, 401(k)s, HSAs, and 529 plans, you can reduce your tax liability, accelerate your savings, and optimize your investments. Remember to contribute the maximum allowed, diversify your investments, regularly review and rebalance your portfolio, and consider tax-efficient strategies like tax-loss harvesting and Roth conversions. Seeking professional guidance can further enhance your understanding and help you make informed decisions. By making the most of tax-efficient accounts, you can pave the way to a financially secure future and achieve your long-term goals.

22. Leverage the power of compound interest by starting to invest early.

By starting to invest early and harnessing the power of compounding, you can set yourself up for a prosperous future. We will explore the concept of compound interest, its benefits, and practical tips for leveraging it to achieve personal economic growth.

Understanding Compound Interest:

Compound interest is the interest earned on the initial amount of money invested, as well as on the accumulated interest from previous periods. In simpler terms, it's interest on top of interest. The key to maximizing compound interest is time. The earlier you start investing, the longer your money has to grow and compound, resulting in significant wealth accumulation over time.

Benefits of Starting Early:

1. **Accelerated Growth**: By starting to invest early, you give your investments more time to grow. The longer your money is invested, the more it can take advantage of compounding. Over time, compounding can lead to exponential growth and significantly increase the value of your investments.

2. **Time to Weather Market Volatility**: Investing early provides you with more time to weather market fluctuations and economic cycles. While short-term volatility is a natural part of the investment landscape, the long-term trend of the market tends to be upward. By staying invested and riding out market downturns, you can benefit from the overall growth of the market.

3. **Reduced Financial Stress**: Investing early allows you to build a robust financial foundation. As your investments grow over time, you can accumulate wealth and have more financial security. This can help alleviate financial stress and provide peace of mind, knowing that you are actively working towards your long-term financial goals.

Tips for Leveraging Compound Interest:

1. **Start Now**: The most important step is to start investing as soon as possible. Even small amounts invested consistently over time can have a significant impact due to the power of compounding. Don't wait for the "perfect" moment; the earlier you begin, the better.

2. **Take Advantage of Tax-Advantaged Accounts**: Utilize tax-advantaged investment accounts such as IRAs, 401(k)s, or similar retirement plans. These accounts offer tax benefits, such as tax-deferred growth or tax-free withdrawals, depending on the account type. Maximize your contributions to these accounts to optimize the benefits of compound interest.

3. **Diversify Your Investments**: Spread your investments across different asset classes, such as stocks, bonds, and real estate, to mitigate risk and maximize potential returns. Diversification can help protect your investments during market downturns and ensure long-term growth.

4. **Stay Consistent**: Consistency is key when it comes to investing. Make it a habit to invest regularly, whether it's monthly, quarterly, or annually. Automatic contributions or direct deposit into investment accounts can help you stay consistent and disciplined in your approach.

5. **Reinvest Dividends and Returns**: Reinvesting dividends and investment returns can amplify the power of compound interest. Instead of cashing out dividends or taking profits, reinvest them back into your portfolio. This allows your investments to compound even faster.

6. **Stay Informed and Seek Professional Advice**: Stay informed about market trends, investment strategies, and financial news. Consider reading books, articles, and attending educational seminars to enhance your financial knowledge. Additionally, seeking advice from a financial advisor

can provide valuable insights and personalized guidance based on your specific financial goals.

7. **Stay the Course**: Investing is a long-term journey, and it's essential to stay the course, especially during periods of market volatility. Avoid making impulsive investment decisions based on short-term market movements. Stick to your investment plan and remain focused on your long-term objectives.

Insights from Renowned Experts:

1. **Warren Buffett**: Warren Buffett, one of the world's most successful investors, emphasizes the power of compound interest and the importance of starting to invest early. He advises individuals to begin investing as soon as possible to take advantage of the compounding effect over time. Buffett believes that starting early allows investments to grow exponentially and significantly increase wealth in the long run.

2. **Peter Lynch**: Peter Lynch, a legendary investor and author of "*One Up On Wall Street*" stresses the significance of starting to invest early to benefit from the magic of compounding. He encourages individuals to invest in quality companies and hold onto their investments for the long term. Lynch believes that starting early and staying invested can yield significant returns due to the compounding of earnings.

Other Book Examples:

1. "*The Little Book of Common Sense Investing*" by **John C. Bogle**: John C. Bogle, the founder of Vanguard Group, advocates for long-term investing and the power of compounding. He emphasizes the importance of starting to invest early and consistently. Bogle's book provides insights into low-cost index fund investing as a strategy to benefit from long-term market growth and compounding returns.

2. "*The Intelligent Investor*" by **Benjamin Graham**: Benjamin Graham, considered the father of value investing, discusses the concept of compounding in his book. He stresses the importance of long-term investing and starting early to maximize the power of compounding. Graham's book offers valuable insights into value investing strategies and the benefits of patient investing.

Conclusion: Harnessing the power of compound interest through early investing is a game-changer for personal economic growth, finance, and management. By starting to invest early, you give your money more time to grow and compound, setting the stage for long-term wealth accumulation. Remember to start now, take advantage of tax-advantaged accounts, diversify your investments, stay consistent, reinvest dividends and returns, stay informed, seek professional advice when needed, and stay the course. By following these principles, you can unlock the potential of compound interest and pave the way for a financially successful future.

23. Network and build relationships for career and financial opportunities.

Building meaningful relationships can open doors to career opportunities, partnerships, and financial success. We will explore the importance of networking, practical tips for building a strong network, and how it can positively impact your professional and financial life.

The Value of Networking:

1. **Access to Opportunities**: Networking allows you to expand your professional circle and tap into a wide range of career opportunities. Through connections, you can learn about job openings, get referrals, and gain insights into industries or companies that interest you. Building a strong network increases your chances of discovering hidden opportunities that may not be publicly advertised.

2. **Knowledge and Expertise Sharing**: Networking provides an opportunity to learn from others and gain valuable insights. By connecting with professionals in different fields or industries, you can exchange knowledge, best practices, and industry trends. This knowledge-sharing can enhance your own expertise and keep you informed about the latest developments in your field.

3. **Support and Mentorship**: Networking allows you to build a support system of like-minded individuals who can offer guidance, advice, and mentorship. Having mentors and experienced professionals in your network can provide valuable insights and help you navigate challenges or decisions in your career or financial journey.

Tips for Effective Networking:

1. **Be Genuine and Authentic**: When networking, be yourself and approach conversations with authenticity. People appreciate genuine connections and are more likely to engage with you when they sense sincerity. Show interest in others, listen actively, and be respectful of their time and expertise.

2. **Attend Industry Events and Conferences**: Make an effort to attend industry events, conferences, and professional meetups related to your field. These gatherings provide excellent opportunities to meet professionals in your industry and expand your network. Be proactive in introducing yourself, engaging in conversations, and exchanging contact information.

3. **Utilize Online Networking Platforms**: In today's digital age, online networking platforms are invaluable for connecting with professionals worldwide. Platforms like LinkedIn offer a powerful medium to build and maintain your professional network. Create a compelling profile, actively engage with others' content, join industry-specific groups, and reach out to professionals whose expertise aligns with your interests.

4. **Offer Value and Build Relationships**: Networking is not just about taking; it's also about giving. Be generous with your knowledge, skills, and resources. Offer assistance, share valuable information, or connect people who could benefit from each other's expertise. Building relationships based on mutual respect and support can lead to long-lasting connections.

5. **Follow Up and Stay Connected**: After meeting someone new, it's crucial to follow up and maintain the relationship. Send a personalized message or email to express your appreciation for the conversation and express interest in staying connected. Regularly engage with your network by sharing relevant articles, congratulating them on achievements, or attending networking events they organize.

6. **Join Professional Associations and Groups**: Membership in industry-specific associations and groups can provide access to a community of professionals with shared interests. These associations often organize networking events, conferences, and educational programs. Engaging in such associations allows you to establish connections and stay updated on industry developments.

7. **Be a Resource for Others**: Actively seek opportunities to help others within your network. Offer support, share your expertise, or provide introductions when appropriate. By being a resource for others, you strengthen your reputation and build goodwill within your network.

Networking can have a significant impact on both your career and financial success:

1. **Career Growth**: A strong network can help you access job opportunities, gain mentorship, and expand your industry knowledge. It increases your

visibility within your field and enhances your professional reputation. Networking can lead to promotions, career advancements, and opportunities for professional development.

2. **Business and Entrepreneurial Ventures**: Building a network is crucial for entrepreneurs and business owners. It can help you find potential clients, partners, investors, or advisors. Connections within your industry or related fields can provide valuable insights and support as you navigate the challenges of starting and growing a business.

3. **Financial Opportunities**: Networking can uncover financial opportunities such as investment prospects, joint ventures, or partnerships. Being well-connected can give you access to potential investors or financial advisors who can help you make informed decisions regarding your personal finance and investment strategies.

Insights from Renowned Experts:

1. **Keith Ferrazzi**: Keith Ferrazzi, author of "*Never Eat Alone*" emphasizes the importance of networking and building relationships for career and financial opportunities. He believes that developing a strong professional network can open doors to new job opportunities, business ventures, and financial growth. Ferrazzi advises individuals to prioritize relationship-building and to offer value to others without expecting immediate returns.

2. **Dale Carnegie**: Dale Carnegie, author of "*How to Win Friends and Influence People*" stresses the significance of building genuine relationships for both personal and financial success. He highlights the importance of effective communication, active listening, and showing genuine interest in others. Carnegie believes that building strong relationships creates a network of support and opens doors to valuable opportunities.

Other Book Examples:

1. "*Give and Take*" by **Adam Grant**: Adam Grant's book explores the concept of reciprocity and the benefits of giving to others. He argues that building relationships based on generosity and helping others can lead to long-term success and financial opportunities. Grant provides insights into how a giving mindset can create a network of supportive connections that can enhance both personal and financial growth.

2. "*The Go-Giver*" by **Bob Burg** and **John David Mann**: This book tells a parable about the power of giving and building relationships. It emphasizes the idea that success comes from adding value to others' lives. The authors

illustrate how cultivating strong relationships and creating a network of trusted connections can lead to financial abundance and career opportunities.

Conclusion: Networking is a powerful tool for personal economic growth, finance, and management. By actively building and nurturing relationships, you open doors to career opportunities, gain valuable knowledge, find support and mentorship, and access financial prospects. Embrace networking as an ongoing practice and approach it with sincerity, authenticity, and a willingness to help others. Your network is a valuable asset that can fuel your success in both business and life. Start networking today and unlock the doors to a world of possibilities.

24. Learn about personal tax strategies to minimize tax liabilities.

You can optimize your financial situation, minimize tax liabilities, and keep more of your hard-earned money. We will explore various tax-saving strategies that can help you win in business and life while complying with tax laws.

Importance of Personal Tax Strategies:

1. **Maximizing Income**: Personal tax strategies allow you to optimize your income by reducing the amount of tax you owe. By minimizing your tax liabilities, you have more disposable income to invest, save, or use for personal goals.

2. **Financial Planning**: Incorporating tax strategies into your financial planning enables you to make informed decisions regarding investments, retirement planning, and major purchases. By considering the tax implications of your financial moves, you can align your goals with tax-efficient strategies.

3. **Legal Compliance**: Understanding tax laws and regulations is essential to ensure you comply with legal requirements. By staying informed, you can avoid penalties, audits, and other complications that may arise from non-compliance.

Key Personal Tax Strategies:

1. **Take Advantage of Tax-Advantaged Accounts**: Explore and utilize tax-advantaged accounts such as Individual Retirement Accounts (IRAs), 401(k) plans, Health Savings Accounts (HSAs), and Flexible Spending Accounts (FSAs). These accounts offer tax benefits, such as tax-deferred

growth, tax deductions, or tax-free withdrawals, depending on the account type and purpose.

2. **Deductible Expenses**: Familiarize yourself with deductible expenses that can lower your taxable income. Examples include mortgage interest, student loan interest, medical expenses, state and local taxes, and certain business expenses if you're self-employed. Keep accurate records and consult with a tax professional to ensure you claim eligible deductions.

3. **Tax-Efficient Investments**: Consider tax-efficient investment strategies, such as investing in tax-efficient funds, tax-free municipal bonds, or utilizing tax-loss harvesting to offset capital gains with capital losses. These strategies can help minimize taxable investment income.

4. **Utilize Tax Credits**: Take advantage of available tax credits, as they directly reduce your tax liability. Examples include the Earned Income Tax Credit (EITC), Child Tax Credit, and education-related credits like the Lifetime Learning Credit or the American Opportunity Tax Credit. Ensure you meet the eligibility criteria and claim the credits you're entitled to.

5. **Capital Gains and Losses**: Understand how capital gains and losses affect your taxes. Long-term capital gains generally have lower tax rates than short-term gains. Consider holding investments for more extended periods to qualify for lower tax rates. Additionally, offsetting capital gains with capital losses can help reduce your overall tax liability.

6. **Consider Tax Filing Status**: Evaluate your tax filing status to determine the most advantageous option for your situation. Married couples can choose between filing jointly or separately, and sometimes one option may result in lower taxes. Analyze your circumstances, consult with a tax advisor, and choose the filing status that optimizes your tax situation.

7. **Plan Charitable Contributions**: Charitable donations can offer tax benefits while supporting causes you care about. Research eligible charitable organizations, keep records of your donations, and consider maximizing deductions by grouping contributions in a particular tax year.

8. **Stay Informed and Seek Professional Advice**: Tax laws and regulations change regularly, so it's important to stay updated on the latest developments. Consider consulting with a qualified tax professional who can provide personalized guidance based on your specific financial situation.

Insights from Renowned Experts:

1. **Robert Kiyosaki**: Robert Kiyosaki, author of "*Rich Dad Poor Dad*" emphasizes the importance of learning about personal tax strategies to minimize tax liabilities. He believes that understanding the tax system and implementing effective strategies can have a significant impact on an individual's financial well-being. Kiyosaki encourages individuals to educate themselves about tax laws and seek professional advice to legally reduce their tax burdens.

2. **Mark J. Kohler**: Mark J. Kohler, a tax and legal expert and author of "*What Your CPA Isn't Telling You*" stresses the significance of learning personal tax strategies. He advises individuals to be proactive in their tax planning and take advantage of available deductions, exemptions, and credits. Kohler believes that by learning about tax strategies, individuals can optimize their financial situation and keep more money in their pockets.

3. **Tom Wheelwright**: Tom Wheelwright, author of "*Tax-Free Wealth*" stresses the significance of understanding personal tax strategies to minimize tax liabilities. He advocates for proactive tax planning and taking advantage of tax incentives provided by the government. Wheelwright believes that by utilizing legitimate tax strategies, individuals can reduce their tax burdens and redirect those savings towards wealth-building activities.

Other Book Examples:

1. "*Lower Your Taxes - BIG TIME!*" by **Sandy Botkin**: Sandy Botkin's book focuses on practical tax strategies that individuals can use to lower their tax liabilities. He provides tips on maximizing deductions, taking advantage of tax breaks, and leveraging tax planning opportunities. Botkin's book aims to empower individuals with knowledge and strategies to minimize their taxes.

2. "*The Tax and Legal Playbook*" by **Mark J. Kohler**: Mark J. Kohler's book focuses on tax and legal strategies for individuals and small business owners. He provides practical advice on minimizing tax liabilities through proper planning, deductions, and entity structuring. Kohler's book aims to empower readers with knowledge and strategies to optimize their tax situations.

Conclusion: Learning about personal tax strategies is a valuable skill for personal economic growth, finance, and management. By understanding the intricacies of

Theia Stewart
Member of PageTitans

I wanted to remind you of the **free gift** that you are welcome to download. There is free additional content.

To download your free copy, simply follow the link or scan the QR code. Please **don't forget to subscribe** to stay in touch with PageTitans.

http://pagetitans.com?page=0000G19

the tax system and implementing tax-saving strategies, you can minimize tax liabilities, maximize your financial resources, and achieve your goals more efficiently. However, it's crucial to stay informed, seek professional advice when needed, and ensure compliance with tax laws. Empower yourself with knowledge and take control of your personal finances through effective tax planning. With the right strategies in place, you can pave the way to financial success and enjoy the rewards of your hard work while keeping your tax burdens at a minimum.

25. Take calculated risks in investment opportunities.

While risk can be intimidating, it is often a necessary element for achieving substantial financial gains. We will explore the importance of taking calculated risks, provide practical tips for assessing investment opportunities, and share real-world examples of successful risk-takers. So, buckle up and get ready to discover the key to winning in both business and life through strategic risk-taking.

Understanding Calculated Risks:

1. **Diversification**: One of the fundamental principles of risk management is diversifying your investment portfolio. By spreading your investments across different asset classes, sectors, and geographic regions, you can mitigate the impact of any single investment's performance on your overall portfolio. Diversification reduces the risk of significant losses and provides an opportunity for potential gains in various market conditions.

2. **Research and Analysis**: Before committing to any investment opportunity, thorough research and analysis are essential. Evaluate the market trends, study the company's financials, and understand the industry dynamics. Assess the potential risks, rewards, and the alignment of the investment opportunity with your financial goals.

3. **Risk-Reward Ratio**: The risk-reward ratio is a critical metric to consider when evaluating investment opportunities. Assess the potential returns against the associated risks. A higher risk-reward ratio indicates a potentially higher return on investment but also comes with greater risk. Consider your risk tolerance and investment objectives to make informed decisions.

4. **Risk Management Strategies**: Alongside taking calculated risks, implementing risk management strategies is vital. Set clear investment goals, determine your risk tolerance, and establish stop-loss orders or exit

strategies to limit potential losses. Regularly review your portfolio and adjust your investments based on changing market conditions.

5. **Knowledge and Education**: Investing in your knowledge and staying informed about the financial markets is crucial for making calculated investment decisions. Attend seminars, read books, follow financial news, and learn from successful investors. Understanding the fundamental principles of investing equips you with the confidence and expertise needed to assess risks effectively.

Tips for Taking Calculated Risks:

1. **Define Your Risk Tolerance**: Understand your risk tolerance by evaluating your financial situation, goals, and personal preferences. Assess how much risk you can comfortably afford to take and align your investment decisions accordingly.

2. **Start Small**: When venturing into new investment opportunities, consider starting with a small allocation of your portfolio. This allows you to test the waters, gain experience, and evaluate the performance before committing more substantial resources.

3. **Seek Professional Advice**: Consult with financial advisors or investment professionals who can provide expert guidance based on your unique circumstances. They can help you assess risks, identify suitable investment options, and develop a well-rounded investment strategy.

4. **Stay Updated and Adaptive**: The investment landscape is dynamic, and market conditions can change rapidly. Stay updated with current economic trends, industry developments, and regulatory changes. Being adaptable and willing to adjust your investment strategy when necessary is crucial for long-term success.

5. **Learn from Failure**: Not all investment decisions will yield positive outcomes. Embrace failures as learning opportunities and analyze the reasons behind them. Understand that even the most successful investors experience setbacks, and it is through these experiences that growth and wisdom emerge.

Real-Life Examples of Successful Risk-Takers:

1. **Warren Buffett**: Known as one of the world's most successful investors, Warren Buffett is renowned for taking calculated risks in the stock market. His investment philosophy focuses on thoroughly researching companies, investing for the long term, and identifying undervalued opportunities.

Buffett's disciplined approach has earned him significant wealth and made him an iconic figure in the investment world.

2. **Elon Musk**: The visionary entrepreneur Elon Musk is known for taking calculated risks with his ventures, such as Tesla and SpaceX. Despite facing numerous challenges, Musk has demonstrated his ability to assess risks, push boundaries, and pursue ambitious goals. His calculated risks have resulted in groundbreaking innovations and substantial financial success.

3. **Jeff Bezos**: The founder of Amazon, Jeff Bezos, took a calculated risk by expanding the company's operations beyond bookselling to become the e-commerce giant it is today. Bezos recognized the potential of online retail and invested heavily in infrastructure, logistics, and technology. His risk paid off, and Amazon became one of the most valuable companies globally.

Book Examples:

1. "*The Intelligent Investor*" by **Benjamin Graham**: Although this book primarily focuses on value investing and risk management, Benjamin Graham emphasizes the importance of taking calculated risks in investment opportunities. He discusses the concept of margin of safety and advises investors to analyze potential investments carefully, considering both the potential rewards and risks involved.

2. "*Thinking, Fast and Slow*" by **Daniel Kahneman**: While this book delves into the field of behavioral economics, it provides valuable insights into decision-making and risk-taking. Daniel Kahneman explores the biases and heuristics that influence our perception of risk and advises readers on how to make more informed and calculated investment decisions.

3. "*Fooled by Randomness*" by **Nassim Nicholas Taleb**: Nassim Nicholas Taleb's book challenges traditional notions of risk and uncertainty in investment. He emphasizes the importance of understanding the role of luck and randomness in investment outcomes and encourages readers to take calculated risks based on a thorough understanding of the underlying probabilities.

4. "*The Warren Buffett Way*" by **Robert G. Hagstrom**: While this book primarily focuses on the investment strategies of Warren Buffett, it provides insights into the approach of one of the most successful investors of our time. Warren Buffett is known for taking calculated risks in

investment opportunities by thoroughly analyzing businesses, assessing their competitive advantages, and seeking favorable risk-reward ratios.

Conclusion: Taking calculated risks in investment opportunities is a vital aspect of personal economic growth, finance, and management. By diversifying your portfolio, conducting thorough research, managing risks effectively, and continuously learning, you can increase your chances of achieving significant financial gains. Remember to align your risk tolerance with your investment objectives, seek professional advice when needed, and stay adaptable in the ever-changing investment landscape. Taking calculated risks is a path towards unlocking new possibilities, realizing your financial goals, and ultimately winning in both business and life.

Remember, fortune favors the brave, but it rewards those who approach risk with careful consideration and strategic planning. So, embrace calculated risks, seize investment opportunities, and embark on your journey to personal and financial prosperity.

26. Invest in yourself through personal development and self-improvement.

By nurturing your skills, expanding your knowledge, and fostering personal growth, you create a solid foundation for achieving success in various aspects of your life. We will explore the importance of investing in yourself, provide practical tips for personal development, and draw inspiration from notable figures and influential books. So, let's dive in and discover the transformative power of self-investment.

The Power of Personal Development:

1. **Continuous Learning**: The pursuit of knowledge is a lifelong journey that propels personal and professional growth. Invest in books, online courses, workshops, and seminars that align with your interests and goals. Engage in self-study, explore new subjects, and develop a thirst for knowledge that drives your personal development forward.

2. **Develop Transferable Skills**: Identify key skills that are relevant to your desired field or industry. These skills, such as communication, problem-solving, leadership, and adaptability, are transferable across different domains. Strengthening these skills through training, practice, and real-world experiences enhances your marketability and opens doors to new opportunities.

3. **Set Meaningful Goals**: Goal setting is a powerful tool for personal and professional growth. Define clear, specific, and achievable goals that resonate with your passions and aspirations. Break them down into actionable steps and monitor your progress. Regularly reassess and adjust your goals to stay aligned with your evolving vision.

4. **Emotional Intelligence**: Emotional intelligence (EQ) plays a significant role in personal and professional success. Invest in developing your EQ by cultivating self-awareness, empathy, and effective communication. Enhancing your emotional intelligence empowers you to navigate relationships, manage conflicts, and lead with empathy and authenticity.

Practical Tips for Personal Development:

1. **Create a Personal Development Plan**: Outline your areas of focus, set specific goals, and develop a plan for personal development. Identify the resources, courses, mentors, or coaches that can assist you in your journey. Regularly review and update your plan to ensure continuous progress.

2. **Embrace a Growth Mindset**: Cultivate a growth mindset that embraces challenges, views failure as an opportunity to learn, and believes in the power of effort and perseverance. A growth mindset fosters resilience, adaptability, and a hunger for continuous improvement.

3. **Seek Mentors and Role Models**: Surround yourself with mentors and role models who inspire and challenge you. Learn from their experiences, seek guidance, and observe their success strategies. Mentors can provide valuable insights, advice, and support as you navigate your personal and professional journey.

4. **Take Care of Your Well-being**: Personal development encompasses physical, mental, and emotional well-being. Prioritize self-care, maintain a healthy lifestyle, and cultivate positive habits. Engage in activities that reduce stress, enhance creativity, and promote overall well-being.

Learning from the Greats:

1. **Benjamin Franklin**: Benjamin Franklin was an advocate of personal development and self-improvement. His autobiography, "*The Autobiography of Benjamin Franklin*" serves as a timeless guide to self-mastery. Franklin's emphasis on virtues, self-discipline, and lifelong learning inspires individuals to invest in themselves for personal and economic growth.

2. **Oprah Winfrey**: Oprah Winfrey, one of the most influential media moguls, is a strong advocate for personal development. Her book club and motivational content encourage individuals to embrace self-reflection, expand their perspectives, and continuously learn and grow.

3. "*The 7 Habits of Highly Effective People*" by **Stephen R. Covey**: This renowned book outlines seven habits that are instrumental in personal and professional success. Covey emphasizes principles such as proactive behavior, goal setting, effective communication, and synergy, providing actionable strategies for self-improvement and personal growth.

Conclusion: Investing in yourself through personal development and self-improvement is a transformative journey that empowers you to reach your full potential, achieve personal economic growth, and lead a fulfilling life. By nurturing your skills, expanding your knowledge, setting meaningful goals, and learning from the wisdom of influential figures and books, you embark on a path of continuous growth and self-discovery. Remember, success is not merely measured by external achievements but also by the growth and fulfillment you experience along the way.

Invest in yourself, for you are your greatest asset. Embrace the power of personal development, seize opportunities for learning and growth, and embark on a lifelong journey of self-investment. As you evolve, your personal economic growth, finance, and management skills will flourish, enabling you to not only win in business but also thrive in all aspects of life.

27. Avoid unnecessary fees and charges by choosing low-cost financial products.

One area where individuals often overlook potential savings is in the realm of fees and charges associated with financial products. We will explore the importance of avoiding unnecessary fees and charges, provide practical tips for selecting low-cost financial products, and draw inspiration from notable figures and renowned books that shed light on this topic. So, let's dive in and uncover the secrets to optimizing your financial journey.

Understanding the Impact of Fees and Charges:

Fees and charges are expenses that financial institutions and service providers levy on their customers for various services and products. These costs can range from transaction fees, account maintenance fees, investment management fees, credit card fees, to high interest rates. While some fees are inevitable, minimizing unnecessary charges can significantly impact your financial well-being and contribute to your economic growth.

Practical Tips for Choosing Low-Cost Financial Products:

1. **Research and Compare**: Before engaging with any financial institution or service provider, take the time to research and compare fees and charges associated with their products. Pay attention to annual maintenance fees, transaction costs, and any hidden charges that might apply. Online resources and comparison platforms can assist you in evaluating different options.

2. **Consider Passive Investing**: Consider incorporating passive investing strategies, such as index funds and exchange-traded funds (ETFs), into your investment portfolio. These investment vehicles typically have lower expense ratios compared to actively managed funds, reducing the impact of fees on your long-term returns.

3. **Review Banking Services**: Regularly review the fees associated with your banking services, including account maintenance fees, ATM fees, and overdraft charges. Look for banks that offer low or no-cost accounts, ATM fee reimbursements, and other perks that align with your financial needs.

4. **Credit Cards**: Be mindful of credit card fees, such as annual fees, foreign transaction fees, and late payment fees. Select credit cards that offer favorable terms, rewards, and minimal charges. Paying your credit card balance in full each month can help you avoid interest charges and additional fees.

5. **Investment Accounts**: When selecting investment accounts, such as Individual Retirement Accounts (IRAs) or brokerage accounts, compare the fee structures of different providers. Look for institutions that offer low-cost or commission-free trading options to minimize transaction fees.

6. **Loan Products**: When borrowing, pay attention to interest rates, origination fees, and prepayment penalties. Compare loan offers from different lenders to ensure you are obtaining the most favorable terms and minimizing unnecessary costs.

7. **Seek Professional Advice**: If you require assistance with complex financial matters, seek advice from a fee-only financial advisor. Fee-only advisors charge a transparent fee for their services, eliminating potential conflicts of interest associated with commission-based compensation.

Famous Figures and Books on Financial Management:

1. **John Bogle**: John Bogle, the founder of Vanguard Group, advocated for low-cost investing and is renowned for his philosophy of index fund investing. His book, *"The Little Book of Common Sense Investing"* emphasizes the importance of minimizing fees and charges by investing in low-cost index funds. Bogle's approach has resonated with millions of investors worldwide.

2. **Warren Buffett**: Warren Buffett, one of the most successful investors of our time, has consistently highlighted the importance of fees and charges in investment decisions. Buffett advises individuals to steer clear of high-cost mutual funds and actively managed portfolios, which can erode long-term returns. His approach aligns with the notion that minimizing fees and charges can significantly impact investment outcomes.

3. *"The Little Book of Common Sense Investing"* by **John C. Bogle**: In this book, John C. Bogle explains the concept of low-cost investing and the benefits of index funds. He emphasizes the detrimental impact of fees and charges on investment returns and provides practical advice on how to choose low-cost financial products. Bogle's book serves as a guide for individuals seeking to optimize their investment strategies and minimize unnecessary expenses.

Conclusion: Avoiding unnecessary fees and charges is a key strategy for personal economic growth and financial management. By selecting low-cost financial products, you can minimize expenses and maximize the potential growth of your wealth. Notable figures like John Bogle and Warren Buffett have emphasized the significance of fees and charges in financial success. By following practical tips such as researching and comparing options, considering passive investing, reviewing banking services, being mindful of credit card fees, optimizing investment accounts, and seeking professional advice, you can take proactive steps towards avoiding unnecessary costs.

Remember, every dollar saved from unnecessary fees and charges is a dollar that can be reinvested, saved, or used for other important financial goals. By being diligent and informed, you can optimize your financial journey and pave the way for long-term economic growth, financial stability, and success in both business and life.

28. Understand and manage your credit score effectively.

Your credit score plays a significant role in various aspects of your financial journey, including loan approvals, interest rates, insurance premiums, and even job applications. We will explore the importance of understanding and managing your credit score, provide practical tips for improving and maintaining a healthy credit score, and draw inspiration from famous individuals and renowned books that shed light on this topic. So, let's embark on this journey to unravel the secrets of credit score success.

The Power of Credit Score:

Your credit score is a numerical representation of your creditworthiness, reflecting your ability to manage and repay debts. It is typically measured using scoring models such as FICO or VantageScore. A high credit score indicates a lower credit risk, making you an attractive borrower to lenders and granting you access to favorable interest rates and financial opportunities.

Practical Tips for Effective Credit Score Management:

1. **Monitor Your Credit**: Regularly check your credit reports from the three major credit bureaus (Equifax, Experian, and TransUnion) to ensure accuracy and identify any potential errors or fraudulent activities. You are entitled to a free annual credit report from each bureau, which can be obtained through AnnualCreditReport.com.

2. **Pay Bills on Time**: Payment history is a crucial factor in calculating your credit score. Make it a priority to pay your bills, including credit card balances, loans, and utilities, on time. Consider setting up automatic payments or reminders to avoid missing deadlines.

3. **Reduce Credit Card Debt**: High credit card balances can negatively impact your credit utilization ratio, which measures the amount of available credit you are using. Aim to keep your credit card balances low and pay off any outstanding debts as quickly as possible.

4. **Diversify Your Credit Mix**: Having a mix of different types of credit, such as credit cards, installment loans, and a mortgage, can positively impact your credit score. However, only take on credit that you can manage responsibly and avoid overextending yourself.

5. **Limit New Credit Applications**: Each time you apply for new credit, a hard inquiry is placed on your credit report, which can temporarily lower your credit score. Be selective when applying for new credit and only do so when necessary.

6. **Maintain Long-Term Credit Accounts**: Length of credit history is an essential factor in credit scoring models. Keep older credit accounts open, even if they are not actively used, to demonstrate a longer credit history.

7. **Manage Debt-to-Income Ratio**: Lenders consider your debt-to-income ratio, which compares your monthly debt obligations to your income, when evaluating loan applications. Aim to keep this ratio as low as possible by managing your debt responsibly and avoiding excessive borrowing.

8. **Seek Professional Guidance**: If you find yourself struggling with credit issues or have complex financial situations, consider consulting with a reputable credit counselor or financial advisor who can provide guidance tailored to your specific needs.

Insights from renowned experts:

1. **Suze Orman**: Suze Orman is a personal finance expert and author who emphasizes the importance of understanding and managing your credit score effectively. She advises individuals to regularly check their credit reports, pay bills on time, keep credit card balances low, and avoid unnecessary credit applications. Orman believes that a good credit score is crucial for accessing favorable interest rates and securing loans.

2. **Dave Ramsey**: Dave Ramsey, a well-known financial expert and author, stresses the significance of managing your credit score responsibly. He encourages individuals to focus on becoming debt-free and using cash for transactions rather than relying heavily on credit. Ramsey believes that by practicing disciplined spending habits and avoiding unnecessary debt, individuals can build a strong financial foundation.

3. **Farnoosh Torabi**: Farnoosh Torabi, a financial expert and author, highlights the importance of understanding the factors that influence your credit score. She advises individuals to maintain a low credit utilization ratio, avoid closing old credit accounts, and regularly monitor their credit reports. Torabi encourages individuals to be proactive in managing their credit and to address any errors or discrepancies promptly.

Book Examples:

1. *"Your Credit Score: How to Improve the 3-Digit Number That Shapes Your Financial Future"* by **Liz Weston**: In this book, Liz Weston provides insights on understanding and managing your credit score effectively. She explains the factors that influence credit scores, provides strategies for improving them, and offers tips on building a solid credit history. Weston's

book is a practical guide for individuals looking to take control of their credit.

2. "*Credit Repair Kit For Dummies*" by **Steve Bucci**: This book offers practical advice on managing and improving your credit score. Steve Bucci provides step-by-step guidance on understanding credit reports, identifying errors, and implementing strategies to rebuild credit. The book includes useful tips, sample letters, and tools to help individuals navigate the credit repair process.

3. "*The Ultimate Credit Repair Guide: How to Fix, Restore, and Build Your Credit*" by **Robin Leonard** and **John Lamb**: In this comprehensive guide, Leonard and Lamb provide readers with insights into understanding and managing their credit effectively. The book covers topics such as credit reports, credit scoring models, debt management, and strategies for improving credit. It offers practical advice and resources to help individuals take control of their credit.

4. **Dave Ramsey**: Dave Ramsey, a well-known financial author and radio host, advocates for responsible financial management. His book, "*The Total Money Makeover*" delves into the importance of maintaining a good credit score, managing debt, and living a financially healthy life.

Conclusion: Understanding and effectively managing your credit score is a key component of personal economic growth, finance, and management. By implementing the practical tips mentioned above and drawing inspiration from famous individuals and renowned books, you can take control of your credit score and pave the way for financial success. Remember, a healthy credit score opens doors to better loan terms, lower interest rates, and increased financial opportunities. Embrace the power of credit score management and embark on a journey towards personal economic growth and financial well-being.

29. Diversify your investments across different asset classes.

Diversifying your investments across different asset classes can be a powerful strategy that helps mitigate risk, optimize returns, and build long-term wealth. We will explore the importance of diversification, provide insights from famous individuals and renowned books, and offer practical tips on how to diversify your investment portfolio effectively. So, let's embark on this journey to uncover the secrets of successful diversification and how it can propel you towards victory in both business and life.

The Power of Diversification:

Diversification is the practice of spreading your investments across different asset classes, such as stocks, bonds, real estate, and commodities. By doing so, you reduce the concentration of risk in any single investment and increase the potential for long-term growth. This strategy allows you to capture the benefits of various market cycles and cushion the impact of market downturns.

Practical Tips for Effective Diversification:

1. **Assess Your Risk Tolerance**: Before embarking on diversification, it's crucial to evaluate your risk tolerance. Determine the level of risk you are comfortable with and align your investment choices accordingly. Younger individuals with a longer time horizon may have a higher tolerance for risk and can allocate a larger portion of their portfolio to equities.

2. **Understand Asset Classes**: Educate yourself about different asset classes and their characteristics. Stocks offer growth potential, bonds provide income and stability, real estate can offer diversification and income, while commodities can act as a hedge against inflation. By understanding each asset class, you can make informed investment decisions.

3. **Allocate Across Asset Classes**: Allocate your investments across different asset classes based on your risk tolerance, financial goals, and time horizon. A well-diversified portfolio may include a mix of stocks, bonds, real estate investment trusts (REITs), exchange-traded funds (ETFs), and other suitable investment vehicles.

4. **Consider Geographical Diversification**: Expand your diversification strategy by considering investments in different regions or countries. Global diversification can help reduce the impact of regional economic downturns and capture growth opportunities in emerging markets.

5. **Rebalance Regularly**: Regularly review and rebalance your portfolio to maintain your desired asset allocation. Over time, some investments may outperform others, leading to an imbalance. Rebalancing involves selling overweighted assets and buying underweighted ones, ensuring your portfolio stays aligned with your investment goals.

6. **Seek Professional Advice**: If you are new to investing or find the process overwhelming, consider consulting a financial advisor who can provide personalized guidance. A professional can assess your financial situation, risk tolerance, and investment objectives to help you create a diversified portfolio that suits your needs.

7. **Consider Index Funds and ETFs**: Index funds and ETFs are investment vehicles that provide instant diversification by tracking broad market indices. These options offer exposure to multiple stocks or bonds within a single investment, reducing the need for individual security selection.

8. **Practice Patience and Discipline**: Diversification is a long-term strategy, and it requires patience and discipline. Avoid making impulsive investment decisions based on short-term market fluctuations. Stay focused on your financial goals and maintain a long-term perspective.

Insights from renowned experts:

1. **Warren Buffett**: Warren Buffett, one of the most successful investors of all time, emphasizes the importance of diversification in investment portfolios. He advises investors to spread their investments across different asset classes, such as stocks, bonds, real estate, and commodities. Buffett believes that diversification helps reduce risk and provides opportunities for long-term growth.

2. **Ray Dalio**: Ray Dalio, the founder of Bridgewater Associates and a renowned hedge fund manager, also emphasizes the significance of diversification. In his book "*Principles: Life and Work*" Dalio explains his investment philosophy, which includes the concept of diversification. He suggests that investors should allocate their assets across a mix of investments that have low correlations with each other.

3. **Jack Bogle**: Jack Bogle, the founder of Vanguard Group and a pioneer of index fund investing, stresses the importance of diversification for individual investors. In his book "*The Little Book of Common Sense Investing*" Bogle promotes the idea of investing in low-cost index funds that provide broad market exposure across different asset classes. He believes that diversification through index funds is a simple yet effective strategy for long-term investment success.

Other Book Examples:

1. "*A Random Walk Down Wall Street*" by **Burton Malkiel**: In this classic investment book, Malkiel emphasizes the importance of diversification in investment portfolios. He discusses various asset classes and advocates for a balanced and diversified approach to investing. Malkiel explains the benefits of spreading investments across different sectors and asset classes to mitigate risk and improve long-term returns.

2. "*The Intelligent Investor*" by **Benjamin Graham**: Graham, often referred to as the father of value investing, discusses the concept of diversification

in his book. He advises investors to spread their investments across different types of securities and industries to reduce risk. Graham emphasizes the importance of analyzing individual investments and maintaining a well-diversified portfolio.

3. "*The Four Pillars of Investing*" by **William Bernstein**: Bernstein explores the topic of diversification in this book, highlighting its role in reducing risk and enhancing long-term returns. He discusses the benefits of diversifying across asset classes, geographic regions, and investment styles. Bernstein provides practical advice on constructing a diversified investment portfolio that aligns with an individual's goals and risk tolerance.

Conclusion: Diversifying your investments across different asset classes is a powerful strategy for personal economic growth, finance, and management. Famous individuals like Warren Buffett and Benjamin Graham, as well as renowned books, have highlighted the importance of diversification in building wealth and managing risk. By understanding asset classes, assessing your risk tolerance, and allocating your investments wisely, you can create a well-diversified portfolio that enhances your chances of success. Remember to regularly review and rebalance your portfolio, seek professional advice when needed, and maintain discipline throughout your investment journey. Embrace the power of diversification, and let it guide you towards victory in both business and life.

30. Invest in index funds for broad market exposure and low fees.

When it comes to personal economic growth, finance, and management, one of the most effective strategies is to invest in index funds. Index funds offer broad market exposure, low fees, and a simplified approach to investing. We will explore the benefits of index funds, provide insights from famous individuals and renowned books, and offer practical tips on how to leverage index funds to win in both business and life. So, let's dive into the world of index funds and uncover the secrets to unlocking your financial potential.

The Rise of Index Funds:

Index funds have gained significant popularity in recent years, and for good reason. These investment vehicles provide broad market exposure by tracking a specific index, such as the S&P 500 or the FTSE 100. Rather than relying on active stock picking, index funds aim to replicate the performance of the underlying index. This passive approach offers several advantages for personal economic growth and financial management.

Advantages of Index Funds:

1. **Broad Market Exposure**: Index funds allow investors to gain exposure to a diversified portfolio of stocks or bonds across various sectors and industries. This broad market exposure helps spread risk and captures the overall market performance.

2. **Cost Efficiency**: Index funds typically have lower expense ratios compared to actively managed funds. The absence of high management fees and frequent trading activity contributes to the cost efficiency of index funds, allowing investors to keep more of their investment returns.

3. **Simplified Investing**: Index funds offer a straightforward and accessible investment option, making them suitable for both novice and experienced investors. With index funds, you don't need to constantly monitor individual stocks or make complex investment decisions.

4. **Consistency**: Index funds aim to replicate the performance of an index, providing investors with consistent returns over the long term. While they may not outperform the market, they offer stability and align with the belief that time in the market is more important than timing the market.

Tips for Investing in Index Funds:

1. **Determine Your Investment Goals**: Clarify your financial goals and time horizon before investing in index funds. Whether you are saving for retirement or a specific financial milestone, understanding your objectives will help you choose the appropriate index funds.

2. **Research and Select the Right Index Funds**: There are numerous index funds available, each tracking a different index. Conduct thorough research, compare expense ratios, historical performance, and the fund's tracking error to identify the index funds that align with your investment goals.

3. **Consider a Total Market Index Fund**: A total market index fund aims to replicate the performance of the entire stock market, providing broad diversification. This type of index fund can be a solid foundation for your investment portfolio.

4. **Dollar-Cost Averaging**: Implement a systematic investment approach by regularly contributing a fixed amount to your index fund. This strategy,

known as dollar-cost averaging, helps mitigate the impact of market volatility and allows you to buy more shares when prices are lower.

5. **Rebalance Periodically**: Monitor your index fund holdings and rebalance your portfolio periodically to maintain your desired asset allocation. Over time, certain asset classes may outperform others, leading to an imbalance in your portfolio.

6. **Seek Professional Guidance**: If you are unsure about investing in index funds or need assistance in creating a well-diversified portfolio, consider consulting a financial advisor. They can provide personalized advice based on your financial situation and goals.

Insights from renowned experts:

1. **John C. Bogle**: John C. Bogle, the founder of Vanguard Group and a proponent of passive investing, strongly advocated for investing in index funds. He believed that index funds provide broad market exposure and deliver competitive returns over the long term. Bogle's book "*The Little Book of Common Sense Investing*" discusses the benefits of low-cost index funds and highlights the impact of fees on investment returns.

2. **Warren Buffett**: Warren Buffett has also expressed his support for index funds. In his annual shareholder letters and interviews, Buffett has recommended that individual investors consider low-cost index funds as a sensible long-term investment option. Buffett has often stated that low fees and broad market exposure make index funds an attractive choice for the majority of investors.

Other Book Examples:

1. "*A Random Walk Down Wall Street*" by **Burton Malkiel**: In this book, Malkiel explores the efficient market hypothesis and argues in favor of index funds as a reliable investment strategy. He presents evidence that supports the idea that trying to beat the market consistently is challenging and that index funds offer an efficient way to capture market returns.

2. "*The Bogleheads' Guide to Investing*" by **Taylor Larimore**, **Mel Lindauer**, and **Michael LeBoeuf**: This book, written by members of the Bogleheads community, provides practical guidance on investing, with a strong emphasis on index fund investing. It covers various aspects of portfolio construction, including the benefits of broad market exposure, low costs, and long-term investment strategies.

Conclusion: Investing in index funds is a powerful tool for personal economic growth, finance, and management. Famous individuals like John C. Bogle and Warren Buffett have championed the benefits of index fund investing, while books such as "*The Little Book of Common Sense Investing*" have popularized the concept. By gaining broad market exposure, benefiting from cost efficiency, and simplifying your investment approach, you can position yourself for long-term success. Remember to align your investment goals, conduct thorough research, and consider dollar-cost averaging and periodic rebalancing. Whether you are a novice investor or an experienced one, index funds offer a reliable path to achieving your financial aspirations.

31. Stay informed about economic trends and market developments.

Being aware of the latest shifts in the economy and market conditions allows you to make informed decisions, adapt your strategies, and seize opportunities. We will explore the significance of staying informed, provide insights from famous individuals and notable books, and offer practical tips on how to stay abreast of economic trends and market developments to win in both business and life. So, let's dive into the world of knowledge and discover the keys to staying ahead of the game.

The Significance of Staying Informed:

1. **Identifying Opportunities**: Being aware of economic trends and market developments allows you to identify emerging opportunities. Whether it's a new industry on the rise or a market shift that presents favorable conditions, staying informed puts you in a position to capitalize on these opportunities before others.

2. **Mitigating Risks**: Knowledge of economic trends and market developments helps you mitigate risks. By understanding potential downturns or industry challenges, you can adjust your investment strategies or business plans accordingly, reducing the impact of adverse events.

3. **Making Informed Decisions**: Informed decisions are crucial in personal economic growth, finance, and management. By staying up-to-date with economic trends, you can make informed choices regarding investments, career moves, or entrepreneurial ventures, increasing the likelihood of success.

Tips for Staying Informed:

1. **Read Widely**: Engage in regular reading to broaden your knowledge base. Stay updated on financial news, economic reports, and industry-specific publications. Famous books like "The Intelligent Investor" by Benjamin Graham and "A Random Walk Down Wall Street" by Burton Malkiel provide valuable insights into market trends and investment strategies.

2. **Follow Reputable Sources**: Identify reliable sources of economic and market information. Subscribe to reputable financial publications, follow respected economists and analysts on social media platforms, and listen to financial podcasts or watch informative videos from trusted experts.

3. **Attend Conferences and Seminars**: Participate in conferences, seminars, and industry events to gain firsthand knowledge from experts and thought leaders. These events provide insights into emerging trends, disruptive technologies, and market forecasts.

4. **Utilize Financial Tools and Apps**: Take advantage of financial tools and mobile apps that offer real-time market updates, economic indicators, and investment analysis. These tools provide convenient access to information and help you track relevant data for informed decision-making.

5. **Network with Professionals**: Build relationships with professionals in your field of interest. Join industry associations, attend networking events, and engage in discussions with like-minded individuals. Networking provides access to valuable insights and insider perspectives.

6. **Leverage Social Media**: Follow influential individuals, financial institutions, and industry leaders on social media platforms. Twitter, LinkedIn, and specialized forums can be great sources of real-time updates, discussions, and expert opinions.

7. **Seek Professional Advice**: Consider consulting a financial advisor or economist to gain expert guidance tailored to your specific financial goals. They can provide personalized insights and help you navigate complex economic trends.

Insights from Famous Individuals and Books:

1. **Peter Lynch**: Peter Lynch, renowned investor and author of "*One Up on Wall Street*" emphasizes the importance of staying informed and conducting thorough research. He advises investors to "invest in what you know" and to understand the businesses they invest in.

2. **Ray Dalio**: Ray Dalio, the founder of Bridgewater Associates and author of "*Principles*" believes that understanding economic trends is essential for successful investing. He advocates for studying historical patterns and utilizing them to make informed decisions.

3. **Warren Buffett**: Warren Buffett, widely regarded as one of the most successful investors in the world, emphasizes the importance of staying informed about economic trends and market developments. Buffett believes that a thorough understanding of the economic landscape is crucial for making sound investment decisions. He advises investors to stay updated on global economic events, industry trends, and company-specific news to identify opportunities and make informed investment choices.

4. "*The Intelligent Investor*" by **Benjamin Graham**: Although Benjamin Graham is not directly focused on staying informed about economic trends, his book "*The Intelligent Investor*" provides valuable insights on investment principles and strategies. Graham emphasizes the importance of conducting thorough research and analysis before making investment decisions. By studying financial statements, economic indicators, and market trends, investors can gain a better understanding of the investment landscape and make informed choices.

Conclusion: Staying informed about economic trends and market developments is an essential aspect of personal economic growth, finance, and management. By following the advice of famous individuals like Peter Lynch and Ray Dalio and exploring notable books on investing and financial literacy, you can enhance your knowledge and decision-making abilities. Remember to read widely, follow reputable sources, attend conferences, utilize financial tools, network with professionals, leverage social media, and seek professional advice when necessary. With a commitment to staying informed, you can position yourself for success and make informed decisions that contribute to your financial well-being and overall life satisfaction.

32. Practice long-term thinking and avoid emotional investment decisions.

It involves adopting a strategic mindset that focuses on long-term goals rather than short-term gains. By avoiding emotional investment decisions and embracing a patient approach, you can navigate the ups and downs of the financial landscape with confidence. We will explore the importance of long-term thinking, highlight insights from famous individuals and influential books, and provide practical tips on how to cultivate a long-term mindset to win in both business and life.

The Power of Long-Term Thinking:

1. **Overcoming Market Volatility**: Financial markets are inherently volatile, experiencing ups and downs in the short term. By practicing long-term thinking, you can overcome the noise of market fluctuations and focus on the underlying fundamentals of your investments. This approach allows you to ride out temporary setbacks and capitalize on long-term growth potential.

2. **Compound Interest**: Long-term thinking is closely linked to the concept of compound interest, which is the exponential growth of wealth over time. By making consistent, long-term investments, you can harness the power of compounding and significantly increase your wealth over the years. The earlier you start, the greater the benefit.

3. **Avoiding Emotional Decisions**: Emotional investment decisions driven by fear, greed, or short-term market sentiment often lead to suboptimal outcomes. By adopting a long-term perspective, you can distance yourself from these emotional impulses and make rational decisions based on thorough analysis and long-term goals.

Tips for Cultivating a Long-Term Mindset:

1. **Define Your Long-Term Goals**: Clearly identify your long-term financial goals, such as retirement planning, wealth accumulation, or funding education. Having a clear vision of your objectives provides a compass for your decision-making and helps you stay focused during market turbulence.

2. **Create a Diversified Portfolio**: Build a well-diversified investment portfolio that aligns with your long-term goals. A diversified portfolio spreads risk across different asset classes and reduces the impact of short-term market volatility. Consider investing in a mix of stocks, bonds, real estate, and other suitable investments based on your risk tolerance and time horizon.

3. **Develop an Investment Plan**: Establish an investment plan that outlines your long-term strategy. Determine your asset allocation, risk tolerance, and rebalancing strategy. Having a structured plan in place helps you stay disciplined and avoid impulsive decisions during market fluctuations.

4. **Stay Informed but Avoid Overreacting**: Stay updated on market trends and economic developments, but avoid overreacting to short-term news. Remember that long-term investments are driven by fundamental factors rather than daily market noise. Develop a habit of filtering information and focusing on the big picture.

5. **Seek Professional Advice**: Consider consulting a financial advisor who can provide personalized guidance based on your specific financial situation and goals. An experienced advisor can help you develop a long-term investment strategy, provide objective insights, and keep you accountable to your goals.

6. **Practice Patience and Discipline**: Cultivate patience and discipline in your investment approach. Understand that achieving long-term financial goals requires time and perseverance. Avoid chasing quick gains or succumbing to the fear of missing out. Stay committed to your long-term plan, even during periods of market volatility.

Insights from Famous Individuals and Books:

1. **Warren Buffett**: Known as one of the most successful investors in history, Warren Buffett emphasizes the significance of long-term thinking. He famously stated, "The stock market is a device for transferring money from the impatient to the patient." Buffett's investment philosophy centers around holding investments for the long haul and focusing on the intrinsic value of companies.

2. "*The Psychology of Money*" by **Morgan Housel**: This influential book explores the role of human behavior and emotions in financial decision-making. It emphasizes the importance of long-term thinking and avoiding impulsive reactions to short-term market fluctuations.

3. **Peter Lynch**: Peter Lynch, a legendary investor and former manager of the Magellan Fund at Fidelity Investments, is known for his long-term investment approach. He advises investors to practice long-term thinking and avoid making emotional investment decisions. Lynch emphasizes the importance of focusing on the fundamentals of a company and investing in businesses with strong growth potential. He encourages investors to stay disciplined and patient, avoiding the temptation to buy or sell based on short-term market fluctuations.

4. "*The Little Book of Common Sense Investing*" by **John C. Bogle**: John C. Bogle, the founder of Vanguard Group, emphasizes the significance of long-term thinking and avoiding emotional investment decisions in his

book "*The Little Book of Common Sense Investing*" Bogle advocates for passive index investing, where individuals hold a diversified portfolio of low-cost index funds for the long term. By following a disciplined and long-term investment strategy, investors can reduce the impact of short-term market volatility and achieve consistent returns over time.

Conclusion: Practicing long-term thinking is a powerful strategy for personal economic growth, finance, and management success. By learning from the wisdom of famous individuals like Warren Buffett and exploring insightful books like "*The Psychology of Money*" you can cultivate a long-term mindset that helps you navigate the complexities of the financial world. Remember to define your long-term goals, create a diversified portfolio, develop an investment plan, stay informed without overreacting, seek professional advice, and practice patience and discipline. By doing so, you can make informed decisions, withstand short-term market fluctuations, and position yourself for long-term financial prosperity.

33. Invest in your health and well-being for long-term cost savings.

One crucial aspect that is often overlooked is investing in our health and well-being. We will explore the importance of prioritizing our physical and mental well-being, highlight insights from renowned figures and influential books, and provide practical tips on how to invest in our health for long-term cost savings.

The Importance of Investing in Your Health and Well-being:

1. **Long-term Cost Savings**: Investing in your health and well-being can lead to substantial long-term cost savings. By maintaining a healthy lifestyle and proactively managing your health, you can reduce the risk of chronic illnesses, medical expenses, and the need for costly treatments or medications.

2. **Enhanced Productivity and Performance**: When you prioritize your health, you can experience increased energy, improved focus, and heightened productivity. Taking care of your physical and mental well-being allows you to perform at your best, whether it's in your career or personal pursuits.

3. **Improved Quality of Life**: Good health is the foundation for a fulfilling and meaningful life. By investing in your well-being, you can enjoy a higher quality of life, engage in activities you love, and have the energy and vitality to pursue your passions.

Tips for Investing in Your Health and Well-being:

1. **Prioritize Physical Fitness**: Engage in regular physical exercise that suits your preferences and fits into your lifestyle. This could include activities like walking, jogging, swimming, yoga, or joining a sports club. Exercise helps improve cardiovascular health, strengthens muscles, boosts mood, and reduces the risk of various health conditions.

2. **Adopt a Balanced Diet**: Nourish your body with wholesome, nutrient-rich foods. Focus on incorporating fruits, vegetables, whole grains, lean proteins, and healthy fats into your meals. Avoid excessive consumption of processed foods, sugary drinks, and unhealthy snacks. A balanced diet supports overall health, provides essential nutrients, and helps maintain a healthy weight.

3. **Prioritize Sleep**: Establish a consistent sleep routine and ensure you get an adequate amount of restful sleep each night. Quality sleep is crucial for physical and mental rejuvenation, cognitive function, and overall well-being. Create a calming bedtime routine and create an environment that promotes relaxation and rest.

4. **Manage Stress**: Develop effective stress management techniques to maintain your mental well-being. This could include practicing mindfulness, engaging in hobbies or activities that bring you joy, seeking support from friends and family, or seeking professional help if needed. Managing stress can improve your mental clarity, emotional resilience, and overall sense of well-being.

5. **Schedule Regular Health Check-ups**: Stay proactive about your health by scheduling regular check-ups, screenings, and preventive healthcare appointments. This allows for early detection of potential health issues and timely intervention, which can significantly reduce healthcare costs and improve outcomes.

6. **Foster Positive Relationships**: Cultivate meaningful relationships with friends, family, and a supportive community. Social connections are essential for mental and emotional well-being. Surrounding yourself with positive influences, support systems, and uplifting relationships can contribute to a healthier and happier life.

Insights from Renowned Figures and Books:

1. **Benjamin Franklin**: One of the founding fathers of the United States, Benjamin Franklin, famously said, "An ounce of prevention is worth a pound of cure." His emphasis on preventive measures and taking care of

one's health resonates with the idea of investing in our well-being for long-term benefits.

2. "*The Power of Now*" by **Eckhart Tolle**: This bestselling book emphasizes the importance of being present and taking care of our mental and emotional well-being. It highlights the connection between our inner state and our overall quality of life.

Conclusion: Investing in your health and well-being is a vital component of personal economic growth, finance, and management. By drawing inspiration from influential figures like Benjamin Franklin and gaining insights from books like "*The Power of Now*" we recognize the profound impact that prioritizing our health can have on our overall success and happiness. By following practical tips such as prioritizing physical fitness, adopting a balanced diet, managing stress, and scheduling regular health check-ups, we can make a long-term investment in our well-being. Remember, good health is priceless, and by investing in it, we lay the foundation for a thriving and prosperous life.

34. Create a will and establish an estate plan to protect your assets.

When it comes to personal economic growth, finance, and management, many people focus on accumulating wealth and building their assets. However, it is equally crucial to plan for the future and protect what you have worked hard to achieve. Creating a will and establishing an estate plan are essential steps in securing your legacy and ensuring your assets are distributed according to your wishes. We will explore the importance of estate planning, highlight insights from renowned figures and influential books, and provide practical tips on how to create a will and establish an estate plan to safeguard your assets.

The Importance of Estate Planning:

1. **Asset Distribution**: One of the primary benefits of estate planning is ensuring that your assets are distributed according to your wishes. By creating a will, you can designate beneficiaries and specify how your assets should be distributed. Without a will, your assets may be subject to intestacy laws, which may not align with your intentions.

2. **Protecting Loved Ones**: Estate planning goes beyond asset distribution. It allows you to protect your loved ones, especially if you have dependents or family members who rely on your financial support. Through estate

planning, you can establish trusts, appoint guardians for minor children, and provide for their ongoing needs.

3. **Minimizing Estate Taxes**: Proper estate planning can help minimize estate taxes and preserve the value of your assets. By employing various strategies, such as gifting, trusts, and charitable giving, you can optimize your estate plan to reduce the tax burden on your heirs.

4. **Avoiding Probate**: A well-structured estate plan can help your assets avoid probate, which is a lengthy and often expensive legal process. By utilizing tools like trusts, you can transfer assets seamlessly and efficiently to your beneficiaries, bypassing probate court.

Tips for Creating a Will and Establishing an Estate Plan:

1. **Seek Professional Guidance**: Estate planning can be complex, and it is advisable to consult an estate planning attorney who can provide expert guidance tailored to your specific needs. They can help you navigate the legal requirements, tax implications, and intricacies of estate planning.

2. **Take Inventory of Your Assets**: Begin by taking inventory of your assets, including bank accounts, investments, real estate, insurance policies, and valuable possessions. This will help you have a comprehensive understanding of your estate and guide you in making decisions about their distribution.

3. **Determine Your Objectives**: Clarify your objectives for estate planning. Consider who you want to inherit your assets, how you want them to be distributed, and any special considerations or provisions you wish to include. Think about your long-term goals for your assets and the legacy you want to leave behind.

4. **Designate Beneficiaries**: Clearly identify your beneficiaries and designate their specific share of your assets. This ensures that your assets are distributed according to your wishes and avoids potential disputes among family members.

5. **Appoint an Executor**: Select a trusted individual to serve as the executor of your estate. The executor will be responsible for managing the distribution of your assets and ensuring that your wishes are carried out. Choose someone who is reliable, organized, and capable of handling the responsibilities involved.

6. **Consider Trusts**: Depending on your circumstances and goals, establishing trusts can be a valuable component of your estate plan. Trusts

offer flexibility, privacy, and control over the distribution of assets, especially for complex situations or when providing for minor children or individuals with special needs.

7. **Review and Update Regularly**: It is essential to review and update your estate plan periodically, especially after significant life events such as marriage, divorce, the birth of children, or acquiring new assets. Regularly reviewing your plan ensures that it remains current and aligns with your evolving circumstances and objectives.

Insights from Renowned Figures and Books:

1. "*The Wealthy Barber*" by **David Chilton**: This bestselling book emphasizes the importance of estate planning as a critical aspect of personal finance. It stresses that estate planning is not only for the wealthy but for anyone who wants to protect their assets and provide for their loved ones.

2. **Steve Jobs**: The late co-founder of Apple, Steve Jobs, did not leave a will initially, which led to complex legal issues and disputes over his estate. His case serves as a reminder of the importance of having a clear estate plan in place.

Conclusion: Creating a will and establishing an estate plan are critical steps in securing your assets and protecting your loved ones. By drawing insights from influential books like "*The Wealthy Barber*" and learning from real-life examples, such as the case of Steve Jobs, we recognize the importance of estate planning in personal economic growth, finance, and management. Remember to seek professional guidance, take inventory of your assets, determine your objectives, designate beneficiaries, appoint an executor, consider trusts, and review your plan regularly. By taking these proactive steps, you can ensure that your assets are distributed according to your wishes, minimize legal complexities, and leave a lasting legacy for future generations.

35. Understand the power of compounding and the time value of money.

Understanding the power of compounding and the time value of money is essential. These concepts can have a profound impact on our financial well-being over the long term. We will explore the significance of compounding and the time value of money, share insights from influential figures and famous books, and provide practical tips on how to leverage these principles for personal success.

The Power of Compounding:

Compounding refers to the process of generating earnings on both the initial investment and the accumulated interest or returns. Over time, compounding can lead to significant wealth accumulation. Here's how it works:

1. **Time**: Time is a critical factor in compounding. The longer your money remains invested, the more time it has to grow and compound. Starting early gives you a substantial advantage due to the exponential nature of compounding.

2. **Consistency**: Consistently investing and reinvesting your returns allows compounding to work its magic. By reinvesting your earnings, you can accelerate the growth of your investments and harness the power of compounding.

The Time Value of Money:

The time value of money recognizes that money in hand today is worth more than the same amount of money in the future. Here's why:

1. **Inflation**: Inflation erodes the purchasing power of money over time. The value of a dollar today may not be the same in the future due to rising prices and the decreasing value of currency. Therefore, money has greater value when it is available earlier.

2. **Opportunity Cost**: Money has the potential to grow when invested wisely. By delaying investment or savings, you miss out on the opportunity to earn returns and maximize the value of your money.

Practical Tips for Harnessing the Power of Compounding and Time Value of Money:

1. **Start Early**: The earlier you begin investing and saving, the more time your money has to compound and grow. Even small amounts invested consistently over a long period can lead to substantial wealth accumulation.

2. **Invest in Stocks and Bonds**: Historically, stocks and bonds have provided higher returns than traditional savings accounts. By allocating a portion of your investment portfolio to these asset classes, you can take advantage of compounding and the potential for long-term growth.

3. **Automate Investments**: Set up automatic contributions to your investment accounts. By automating your investments, you ensure consistency and eliminate the temptation to deviate from your savings plan.

4. **Reinvest Dividends and Returns**: If you invest in dividend-paying stocks or mutual funds, reinvest the dividends to purchase additional shares. Reinvesting dividends allows you to compound your returns and accelerate wealth accumulation.

5. **Take Advantage of Retirement Accounts**: Maximize your contributions to retirement accounts such as 401(k)s or IRAs. These accounts offer tax advantages and can help your investments grow faster.

6. **Diversify Your Investments**: Spread your investments across different asset classes and sectors to reduce risk. Diversification allows you to capture growth opportunities while mitigating the impact of any individual investment's performance.

7. **Be Patient and Stay Disciplined**: Building wealth through compounding takes time and requires discipline. Stay focused on your long-term financial goals and avoid making impulsive investment decisions based on short-term market fluctuations.

Insights from Influential Figures and Famous Books:

1. **Albert Einstein**: The renowned physicist once referred to compound interest as the "eighth wonder of the world." He understood the exponential growth potential that comes from allowing investments to compound over time.

2. *"The Richest Man in Babylon"* by **George S. Clason**: This classic book imparts timeless financial wisdom through parables and emphasizes the importance of saving, investing, and letting money work for you.

Conclusion: Understanding the power of compounding and the time value of money is crucial for personal economic growth, finance, and management success. Influential figures like Albert Einstein and insightful books like *"The Richest Man in Babylon"* remind us of the transformative potential of compounding. By starting early, remaining consistent, and making strategic investment decisions, we can harness the power of compounding and maximize the value of our money over time. Additionally, recognizing the time value of money emphasizes the importance of acting today and not delaying financial decisions. By incorporating these principles into our financial planning and decision-making, we can set ourselves on a path to long-term financial success and create a brighter future for ourselves.

36. Take steps to minimize investment fees and expenses.

We will explore the significance of minimizing fees and expenses, share insights from renowned individuals and famous books, and provide practical tips on how to reduce costs in your investment journey.

The Impact of Investment Fees and Expenses:

1. **Fee Drag**: Investment fees, such as management fees and expense ratios, eat into your investment returns over time. Even seemingly small percentages can have a significant impact on long-term wealth accumulation.

2. **Compounding Effect**: Just as compounding can work in your favor when it comes to returns, it can also work against you when it comes to fees. High fees can impede the growth potential of your investments and erode your overall returns.

Practical Tips for Minimizing Investment Fees and Expenses:

1. **Choose Low-Cost Investment Vehicles**: Opt for low-cost investment options such as index funds, exchange-traded funds (ETFs), or passively managed mutual funds. These vehicles typically have lower expense ratios compared to actively managed funds.

2. **Compare Expense Ratios**: When selecting funds, compare expense ratios across different options. The expense ratio represents the annual cost of owning the fund as a percentage of your investment. Choose funds with lower expense ratios to minimize costs.

3. **Consider Index Funds**: Index funds are designed to replicate the performance of a specific market index, such as the S&P 500. These funds offer broad market exposure and tend to have lower expense ratios compared to actively managed funds.

4. **Avoid Load Funds**: Load funds are mutual funds that charge a sales commission or load fee. These fees are deducted from your investment upfront or when you sell the fund. Opt for no-load funds to avoid unnecessary expenses.

5. **Look for Fee Waivers or Discounts**: Some investment providers offer fee waivers or discounts based on factors like account size or holding period. Research and compare different providers to identify opportunities for reduced fees.

6. **Consider Direct Investing**: Direct investing platforms allow you to buy and sell stocks or exchange-traded funds directly, bypassing the need for a traditional brokerage account. These platforms often charge lower fees compared to full-service brokerages.

7. **Rebalance Periodically**: Rebalancing your portfolio involves adjusting the allocation of your investments to maintain your desired asset mix. By rebalancing, you can potentially reduce transaction costs and maintain a disciplined investment approach.

8. **Take Advantage of Tax-Efficient Strategies**: High turnover within a fund can lead to increased capital gains taxes. Consider tax-efficient strategies like tax-managed funds or holding investments in tax-advantaged accounts to minimize tax-related expenses.

9. **Seek Professional Advice Wisely**: If you opt for professional investment advice, understand the fee structure and any potential conflicts of interest. Consider fee-only financial advisors who charge a transparent fee for their services, rather than relying on commissions.

10. **Monitor and Review Your Portfolio**: Regularly monitor your investment portfolio and assess the fees and expenses associated with each investment. If certain investments consistently underperform or have high costs, consider making adjustments to optimize your returns.

Insights from Renowned Individuals and Famous Books:

1. **John Bogle**: The late founder of Vanguard Group, John Bogle, emphasized the importance of low-cost investing. His philosophy led to the creation of index funds, which offer broad market exposure at minimal costs.

2. "*A Random Walk Down Wall Street*" by **Burton G. Malkiel**: This classic investment book highlights the advantages of low-cost index funds and warns against the detrimental impact of high fees on investment performance.

Conclusion: Minimizing investment fees and expenses is a crucial aspect of personal economic growth, finance, and management. By implementing strategies such as choosing low-cost investment vehicles, comparing expense ratios, and taking advantage of tax-efficient strategies, you can significantly reduce the impact of fees on your investment returns. Remember the insights from industry pioneers like John Bogle and the wisdom shared in books like "*A Random Walk Down Wall Street*" By taking these steps to minimize fees and expenses, you can unlock the path to financial success, maximize your long-term returns, and achieve your goals in both business and life.

37. Automate bill payments to avoid late fees and penalties.

One way to streamline your financial responsibilities and avoid unnecessary late fees and penalties is to automate your bill payments. Now we will explore the benefits of automating bill payments, share insights from famous individuals, and provide practical tips for implementing this strategy successfully.

Benefits of Automating Bill Payments:

1. **Avoid Late Fees and Penalties**: Late payments can result in hefty fees and penalties, which can significantly impact your finances over time. Automating bill payments ensures that your bills are paid on time, eliminating the risk of incurring unnecessary charges.

2. **Convenience and Time-Saving**: Automating bill payments saves you the hassle of manually paying each bill individually. With automated systems, you can set up recurring payments and free up time for more important tasks.

Practical Tips for Automating Bill Payments:

1. **Create a Budget**: Before setting up automated bill payments, establish a comprehensive budget that outlines your income and expenses. This will help you determine the amount you need to allocate for bill payments each month.

2. **Identify Eligible Bills**: Assess your regular expenses and identify bills that are eligible for automation. Common examples include utility bills, internet and cable services, insurance premiums, mortgage or rent payments, and credit card bills.

3. **Set Up Automatic Payments**: Contact your service providers or financial institutions to set up automatic payments. You can typically do this through their online platforms or by completing a form. Provide the necessary information, such as your bank account details and payment schedule.

4. **Consider Payment Reminders**: If you're concerned about overdrafts or insufficient funds, some bill payment systems offer payment reminder features. These reminders can notify you a few days before the payment is due, allowing you to ensure sufficient funds are available.

5. **Regularly Review Your Statements**: While automating bill payments is convenient, it's essential to review your bank and credit card statements regularly. This helps you identify any discrepancies or errors and ensures that payments are processed correctly.

6. **Maintain a Cash Flow Buffer**: It's wise to maintain a buffer in your checking account to cover unexpected expenses or fluctuations in bill amounts. This helps avoid any potential overdrafts or payment failures.

7. **Update Payment Information**: If you change banks, credit cards, or contact information, promptly update your payment information with the relevant service providers. This ensures a seamless continuation of automated bill payments.

8. **Monitor Billing Changes**: Keep an eye on any changes in billing amounts or due dates. Service providers may adjust billing cycles or rates, and it's essential to stay informed to prevent any surprises or discrepancies in your automated payments.

9. **Retain Control and Flexibility**: While automating bill payments offers convenience, it's crucial to retain control and flexibility over your finances. Regularly review your budget, adjust payment amounts if necessary, and have the option to cancel automated payments if circumstances change.

10. **Stay Vigilant Against Fraud**: Automating bill payments requires providing sensitive financial information. To protect yourself against fraud, ensure you are using secure and reputable payment platforms or systems. Regularly monitor your accounts for any unauthorized activity.

Insights from Famous Individuals and Books:

1. *"The 7 Habits of Highly Effective People"* by **Stephen R. Covey**: This influential book emphasizes the importance of being proactive and organized in managing all aspects of life, including personal finances.

2. **Warren Buffett**: The renowned investor and philanthropist Warren Buffett has frequently highlighted the importance of avoiding unnecessary expenses and being disciplined with financial obligations.

Conclusion: Automating bill payments is a valuable tool for personal economic growth, finance, and management. By setting up automatic payments, you can avoid late fees, penalties, and the stress of managing multiple bills manually. Remember the wisdom shared by renowned individuals like Stephen R. Covey and Warren Buffett, who emphasize the importance of proactive financial management. By implementing the practical tips mentioned above, you can take control of your finances, save time, and focus on more important aspects of your business and life.

38. Evaluate and adjust your investment strategy based on changing market conditions.

The financial markets are dynamic and constantly evolving, thus requiring individuals to evaluate and adjust their investment approach based on changing market conditions. We will explore the importance of evaluating and adjusting your investment strategy, share insights from famous individuals, and provide practical tips for navigating changing market conditions.

The Importance of Evaluating and Adjusting Your Investment Strategy:

1. **Capitalize on Opportunities**: The financial markets are influenced by a multitude of factors, including economic conditions, geopolitical events, and industry trends. By regularly evaluating your investment strategy, you can identify emerging opportunities and make informed decisions to capitalize on them.

2. **Mitigate Risks**: Market conditions can change rapidly, leading to shifts in asset prices and investment risks. By staying vigilant and adjusting your investment strategy accordingly, you can mitigate potential risks and protect your portfolio from adverse market movements.

3. **Optimize Returns**: Evaluating and adjusting your investment strategy allows you to optimize your returns by aligning your portfolio with the most promising investment opportunities. It helps you stay ahead of market trends and position yourself for long-term success.

Practical Tips for Evaluating and Adjusting Your Investment Strategy:

1. **Stay Informed**: Stay updated on market news, economic indicators, and industry trends. Follow reputable financial news sources, read books on investing, and consider subscribing to newsletters or online platforms that provide market insights.

2. **Review Your Investment Goals**: Regularly review your investment goals to ensure they are aligned with your financial objectives. As your circumstances change, such as approaching retirement or saving for a specific goal, adjust your strategy to reflect these new objectives.

3. **Assess Risk Tolerance**: Your risk tolerance may evolve over time. Evaluate your comfort level with risk and adjust your investment strategy accordingly. For example, if you have a lower risk tolerance, consider shifting to more conservative investments.

4. **Diversify Your Portfolio**: Diversification is a fundamental principle of investment management. Evaluate the diversification of your portfolio

across different asset classes, sectors, and geographical regions. Adjust your holdings to maintain a well-balanced and diversified portfolio.

5. **Seek Professional Guidance**: Consider consulting with a financial advisor or investment professional who can provide expert advice tailored to your specific circumstances. They can help you evaluate market conditions and make informed decisions based on your financial goals.

6. **Monitor Investment Performance**: Regularly review the performance of your investments and assess whether they are meeting your expectations. Identify underperforming assets and consider reallocating funds to more promising opportunities.

7. **Be Patient and Avoid Emotional Decisions**: It's essential to maintain a long-term perspective and avoid making impulsive investment decisions based on short-term market fluctuations. Emotions such as fear and greed can cloud judgment, leading to suboptimal outcomes.

8. **Use Tools and Technology**: Leverage technological advancements and investment tools to monitor and evaluate your portfolio. Online platforms and financial apps can provide real-time data, portfolio analysis, and investment recommendations.

9. **Consider Asset Allocation**: Assess the allocation of your assets based on your risk tolerance, investment goals, and market conditions. Adjust the allocation by rebalancing your portfolio periodically to maintain an optimal mix of assets.

10. **Seek Tax Efficiency**: Evaluate the tax implications of your investments and consider tax-efficient strategies such as investing in tax-advantaged accounts or utilizing tax-loss harvesting techniques. Maximizing tax efficiency can enhance your after-tax returns.

Insights from Famous Individuals and Books:

1. **Peter Lynch**: Peter Lynch, a renowned investor and former manager of Fidelity Magellan Fund, is known for his successful investment strategies. His book, "*One Up on Wall Street*" encourages individuals to invest in companies they understand and to stay informed about market developments.

2. **Benjamin Graham**: Known as the father of value investing, Benjamin Graham authored the classic book, "*The Intelligent Investor*" Graham emphasized the importance of evaluating investments based on their

intrinsic value and recommended adjusting strategies to align with changing market conditions.

Conclusion: In the dynamic world of finance and investment, evaluating and adjusting your investment strategy is key to achieving success in business and life. By staying informed, regularly reviewing your portfolio, and adapting to changing market conditions, you can position yourself for long-term growth and optimize your investment returns. Remember the advice of famous investors like Peter Lynch and Benjamin Graham, and remain proactive and flexible in your approach. With careful evaluation and adjustment, you can navigate the ever-changing investment landscape with confidence and achieve your financial goals.

39. Teach children about money management and financial literacy.

Teaching children about money can empower them to make sound financial decisions, cultivate responsible saving and spending habits, and lay the foundation for a successful future. We will explore the importance of teaching children about money management, share insights from experts and famous individuals, and provide practical tips for fostering financial literacy in young minds.

The Importance of Teaching Children About Money Management:

1. **Building a Strong Foundation**: Introducing children to money management at an early age helps establish a solid foundation for their financial future. It enables them to develop healthy attitudes towards money, savings, and responsible spending.

2. **Cultivating Financial Responsibility**: Teaching children about money management cultivates financial responsibility and empowers them to make informed decisions. They learn the value of saving, budgeting, and distinguishing between needs and wants.

3. **Long-Term Financial Well-Being**: Equipping children with financial literacy skills sets them up for long-term financial well-being. They are more likely to develop good saving habits, make wise investment choices, and avoid debt traps later in life.

Practical Tips for Teaching Children About Money Management:

1. **Start Early**: Introduce basic concepts of money management at a young age. Teach them about different denominations, saving, and the importance of setting goals.

2. **Make it Fun and Engaging**: Use age-appropriate games, activities, and real-life examples to make financial education enjoyable. Incorporate hands-on experiences, such as giving them an allowance and encouraging them to save for something they desire.

3. **Lead by Example**: Children often learn by observing their parents' financial behavior. Model responsible financial habits, such as budgeting, saving, and making wise spending choices. Discuss your financial decisions with them to enhance their understanding.

4. **Teach Budgeting Skills**: Help children understand the concept of budgeting by setting up a simple budget for their allowances or earnings. Teach them to allocate money for savings, spending, and charitable contributions.

5. **Encourage Saving**: Emphasize the importance of saving money for short-term goals and long-term aspirations. Introduce them to the concept of compound interest and the benefits of starting to save early.

6. **Introduce Basic Banking**: Teach children about the role of banks, savings accounts, and the concept of earning interest. Take them to the bank to open a savings account and encourage regular deposits.

7. **Teach the Value of Delayed Gratification**: Help children understand that sometimes waiting and saving for something can bring greater satisfaction than immediate impulse purchases. This instills discipline and cultivates patience.

8. **Introduce the Concept of Investing**: As children grow older, introduce them to the concept of investing and the potential for growth and wealth creation. Teach them about stocks, bonds, and other investment options in an age-appropriate manner.

9. **Involve Them in Family Financial Discussions**: Include children in age-appropriate discussions about family finances. This helps them understand how financial decisions are made and encourages them to ask questions.

10. **Encourage Entrepreneurial Thinking**: Foster an entrepreneurial mindset by encouraging children to explore business ideas, start small ventures, or participate in entrepreneurial activities. This nurtures creativity, problem-solving skills, and a sense of financial independence.

Insights from Experts and Famous Individuals:

1. **Warren Buffett**: As one of the world's most successful investors, Warren Buffett has emphasized the importance of financial education. He once

said, "The best investment you can make is in yourself." Buffett believes in equipping children with financial knowledge to set them on a path to long-term success.

2. **Robert Kiyosaki**: Renowned author of "*Rich Dad Poor Dad*" Robert Kiyosaki stresses the significance of teaching children about financial literacy. He advocates for instilling a mindset of financial independence and entrepreneurship, encouraging children to understand the difference between assets and liabilities.

Resources for Teaching Financial Literacy:

1. "*The MoneySmart Family System*" by **Steve and Annette Economides**: This book offers practical strategies for raising financially responsible children and managing family finances effectively.
2. Online Resources: Utilize websites and online platforms that offer interactive games and educational resources focused on teaching financial literacy to children. Some examples include **Money as You Grow**, **Practical Money Skills for Life**, and **Junior Achievement**.

Conclusion: Teaching children about money management and financial literacy is an investment in their future success. By starting early, making it engaging, and incorporating practical lessons, you can equip children with the knowledge and skills needed for responsible financial decision-making. Remember the wisdom of financial experts like Warren Buffett and Robert Kiyosaki, and provide them with resources like books and online platforms to further their financial education. By instilling financial literacy in children, we empower them to navigate the complex world of finance with confidence and set them on a path to win in business and in life.

40. Seek professional advice for complex financial matters.

While we can educate ourselves on various financial topics, complex matters often require the expertise of professionals who specialize in specific fields. So, we will explore the importance of seeking professional advice, share insights from renowned experts, and provide practical tips for finding and working with financial professionals.

The Importance of Seeking Professional Advice:

1. **Specialized Expertise**: Professionals in fields such as financial planning, tax, legal, and investment management possess specialized knowledge and

experience. They stay updated with current regulations, trends, and strategies, which can be invaluable in complex financial matters.

2. **Objective Perspective**: Financial professionals provide an objective viewpoint. They can assess your financial situation impartially and offer recommendations tailored to your specific goals and circumstances. Their expertise helps ensure that emotions and biases do not cloud your judgment.

3. **Comprehensive Financial Planning**: Professionals can help create a comprehensive financial plan that covers various aspects of your financial life, including retirement planning, tax optimization, risk management, estate planning, and investment strategies. They take a holistic approach, considering all relevant factors and aligning your financial decisions with your long-term objectives.

4. **Time and Effort Savings**: Complex financial matters often require extensive research, analysis, and paperwork. By seeking professional advice, you can save time and effort, allowing you to focus on other aspects of your life or business.

Practical Tips for Seeking Professional Advice:

1. **Determine Your Needs**: Before seeking professional advice, identify the specific area in which you require assistance. Whether it's financial planning, tax optimization, investment management, or legal matters, understanding your needs helps you find the right professional.

2. **Research and Credentials**: Conduct thorough research to identify professionals with relevant expertise and credentials in their respective fields. Look for certifications such as Certified Financial Planner (CFP), Certified Public Accountant (CPA), or Chartered Financial Analyst (CFA).

3. **Seek Recommendations**: Ask for recommendations from trusted friends, family members, or colleagues who have had positive experiences with financial professionals. Personal referrals can provide valuable insights and help you find professionals with a proven track record.

4. **Interview Multiple Professionals**: Schedule initial consultations or interviews with multiple professionals to assess their expertise, communication style, and compatibility. Ask about their experience, approach, fees, and how they have helped clients in similar situations.

5. **Fee Structure and Transparency**: Understand the fee structure of the professional you are considering. Some professionals charge a fee based on

an hourly rate, while others may work on a commission basis or charge a percentage of assets under management. Choose a professional who is transparent about their fees and ensures alignment with your budget and expectations.

6. **Communication and Trust**: Clear communication and trust are vital in the client-professional relationship. Ensure that the professional explains complex concepts in a way that is understandable to you and takes the time to address your concerns. Trust your instincts and choose a professional with whom you feel comfortable sharing personal and financial information.

7. **Regular Review and Communication**: Once you have engaged a professional, maintain regular communication and schedule periodic reviews of your financial situation. This ensures that your plan remains aligned with your changing goals, market conditions, and regulatory updates.

Insights from Renowned Experts:

1. **Suze Orman**: As a renowned financial expert and best-selling author, Suze Orman emphasizes the value of seeking professional advice. She once said, "True financial success is not about amassing wealth; it's about having a plan that provides for and protects the people you love."

2. **Peter Lynch**: A legendary investor and former manager of Fidelity Magellan Fund, Peter Lynch encourages individuals to seek professional advice for complex investment decisions. He believes that having an expert guide can help navigate the complexities of the market.

Famous Books on Seeking Professional Advice:

1. "*The Only Investment Guide You'll Ever Need*" by **Andrew Tobias**: This book provides valuable insights into seeking professional advice, selecting financial professionals, and making sound financial decisions.

2. "*The Millionaire Next Door*" by **Thomas J. Stanley** and **William D. Danko**: While this book primarily focuses on wealth accumulation, it highlights the importance of seeking advice from professionals in achieving financial success.

Conclusion: In business and in life, seeking professional advice for complex financial matters is a key strategy for success. Renowned experts like Suze Orman and Peter Lynch emphasize the value of professional guidance in areas such as financial planning, tax optimization, and investment management. By leveraging the specialized expertise, objective perspective, and time-saving benefits that professionals offer, you can make informed decisions and achieve your financial goals. Remember to research, seek recommendations, interview multiple professionals, and prioritize effective communication and trust. With the right professionals by your side and insights from books like "*The Only Investment Guide You'll Ever Need*" and "*The Millionaire Next Door*" you can navigate the complexities of finance with confidence and set yourself up for long-term success in business and in life.

41. Plan for retirement and set aside funds for post-work life.

Retirement planning involves setting aside funds and creating a strategy that allows you to maintain your desired lifestyle once you stop working. We will explore the importance of retirement planning, share insights from renowned experts, and provide practical tips for effectively planning and saving for your post-work life.

The Importance of Retirement Planning:

1. **Maintaining Lifestyle**: Retirement planning ensures that you can maintain your desired lifestyle after you stop working. It helps you avoid financial hardships and provides a sense of security and peace of mind during your retirement years.

2. **Longer Life Expectancy**: With advancements in healthcare and a higher life expectancy, retirement can span several decades. Adequate planning allows you to cover your expenses and enjoy your post-work life without financial constraints.

3. **Social Security Limitations**: Relying solely on social security benefits may not be sufficient to sustain your desired lifestyle. By planning and saving for retirement, you can supplement your social security income and have greater financial freedom.

Practical Tips for Retirement Planning:

1. **Start Early**: Time is your greatest asset when it comes to retirement planning. The earlier you start saving and investing, the more time your money has to grow through compounding. Even small contributions made consistently over a long period can have a significant impact.

2. **Set Clear Retirement Goals**: Determine your retirement goals and estimate the amount of money you will need to sustain your desired lifestyle. Consider factors such as living expenses, healthcare costs, travel,

and hobbies. Having a specific target in mind will help you plan and save effectively.

3. **Maximize Retirement Accounts**: Take advantage of tax-advantaged retirement accounts such as 401(k)s or individual retirement accounts (IRAs). Contribute the maximum amount allowed and consider taking advantage of employer matching contributions. These accounts offer tax benefits and can help grow your retirement savings.

4. **Diversify Investments**: Diversify your retirement investments across different asset classes to mitigate risk and maximize returns. Consider a mix of stocks, bonds, and other investment vehicles that align with your risk tolerance and long-term goals. Seek professional advice or explore investment books like "The Bogleheads' Guide to Retirement Planning" by Taylor Larimore for guidance.

5. **Monitor and Adjust**: Regularly review your retirement plan and make adjustments as needed. Assess your progress, update your projections, and make necessary changes to your savings and investment strategies based on changes in your financial situation and market conditions.

6. **Consider Long-Term Care**: Long-term care costs can significantly impact your retirement savings. Evaluate the need for long-term care insurance or explore other options for covering potential healthcare expenses during retirement.

7. **Seek Professional Advice**: Consult with a financial advisor or retirement planner to ensure that your retirement plan is on track. They can provide guidance on investment strategies, tax-efficient withdrawals, and optimizing your retirement income.

Insights from Renowned Experts:

1. **Warren Buffett**: As one of the most successful investors in the world, Warren Buffett emphasizes the importance of retirement planning. He once said, "Someone's sitting in the shade today because someone planted a tree a long time ago."

2. **Robert Kiyosaki**: Best-selling author and entrepreneur Robert Kiyosaki believes that retirement planning is crucial for financial independence. He stresses the importance of building passive income streams to support your desired lifestyle in retirement.

Famous Books on Retirement Planning:

1. "*The Total Money Makeover*" by **Dave Ramsey**: While this book covers various aspects of personal finance, it offers practical advice on retirement planning, debt management, and building wealth.

2. "*How to Retire Happy, Wild, and Free*" by **Ernie J. Zelinski**: This book focuses on achieving a fulfilling retirement by exploring non-financial aspects such as lifestyle choices, personal development, and finding purpose.

Conclusion: Planning for retirement is essential for personal economic growth and long-term financial security. By starting early, setting clear goals, maximizing retirement accounts, diversifying investments, and regularly monitoring your plan, you can pave the way for a comfortable post-work life. Seek inspiration from renowned experts like Warren Buffett and Robert Kiyosaki and explore books such as "*The Total Money Makeover*" and "*How to Retire Happy, Wild, and Free*" for additional insights. Remember, retirement planning is not a one-time task but an ongoing process that requires periodic review and adjustments. With careful planning and the right strategies in place, you can confidently embrace your post-work life and enjoy the fruits of your labor.

42. Continuously educate yourself about personal finance to make informed decisions.

Continuous learning not only equips you with the knowledge and skills to make informed financial decisions but also empowers you to take control of your economic growth, finance, and management. We will explore the importance of ongoing financial education, share insights from renowned experts, and provide practical tips for continuously educating yourself about personal finance.

The Importance of Continuous Financial Education:

1. **Making Informed Decisions**: Financial education provides you with the knowledge and tools to make informed decisions about budgeting, investing, saving, and managing debt. It helps you understand complex financial concepts, evaluate risks, and identify opportunities.

2. **Adapting to Changing Financial Landscape**: The financial world is constantly evolving, with new products, technologies, and regulations emerging. Continuous education keeps you up-to-date with the latest

trends, allowing you to adapt to changing circumstances and make strategic financial choices.

3. **Building Confidence**: Knowledge breeds confidence. By educating yourself about personal finance, you gain the confidence to navigate financial challenges, negotiate better deals, and take calculated risks. This confidence positively impacts your financial well-being and overall success.

Practical Tips for Continuous Financial Education:

1. **Read Books on Personal Finance**: Books are a valuable source of financial knowledge. Explore renowned titles such as "*Rich Dad Poor Dad*" by **Robert Kiyosaki**, "*The Intelligent Investor*" by **Benjamin Graham**, and "*The Millionaire Next Door*" by **Thomas J. Stanley** for insights into wealth creation, investing, and building financial resilience.

2. **Follow Financial Experts and Influencers**: Follow reputable financial experts, economists, and influencers on social media platforms or subscribe to their newsletters. Their insights, tips, and analysis can keep you informed about market trends, investment strategies, and personal finance best practices.

3. **Attend Workshops and Seminars**: Participate in workshops, seminars, and webinars focused on personal finance. Many organizations and financial institutions offer educational programs covering topics such as budgeting, retirement planning, and investment strategies.

4. **Take Online Courses**: Explore online platforms that offer courses on personal finance and investment. Websites like Coursera, Udemy, and Khan Academy provide a wide range of finance-related courses, including budgeting, financial planning, and investing.

5. **Utilize Podcasts and Videos**: Podcasts and video platforms are excellent resources for learning on the go. Find podcasts dedicated to personal finance, investing, and money management. YouTube channels like "**The Financial Diet**" and "**Graham Stephan**" offer valuable insights and tips.

6. **Engage in Financial Communities**: Join online communities or forums where individuals discuss personal finance topics. Participate in discussions, ask questions, and learn from the experiences of others. Examples include **Reddit's personal finance** subreddit or the **Bogleheads** community.

7. **Attend Local Financial Events**: Check for local financial events, conferences, or workshops in your area. These events provide opportunities to network with professionals, gain insights from industry experts, and expand your knowledge base.

8. **Engage with Financial Blogs and Websites**: Follow reputable financial blogs and websites such as **Investopedia**, **NerdWallet**, and **The Balance**. These platforms offer comprehensive resources, articles, and tools to enhance your financial literacy.

9. **Monitor Financial News**: Stay updated with financial news through reliable sources like CNBC, Bloomberg, or Financial Times. Understanding global economic trends, market movements, and policy changes can help you make better financial decisions.

10. **Join Professional Associations**: Consider joining professional associations related to finance, accounting, or investment. These associations often offer educational resources, conferences, and networking opportunities to enhance your financial knowledge.

Insights from Renowned Experts and Books:

1. **Suze Orman**: Suze Orman, a well-known personal finance expert, emphasizes the significance of financial education. She once said, "A big part of financial freedom is having your heart and mind free from worry about the what-ifs of life."

2. **Warren Buffett**: Warren Buffett, one of the world's most successful investors and the chairman and CEO of Berkshire Hathaway, emphasizes the importance of continuous education in personal finance. Buffett believes that investing in knowledge is one of the best investments individuals can make. He encourages people to read extensively and stay updated on financial news, market trends, and investment strategies. Buffett believes that by continuously educating oneself, individuals can make more informed and rational financial decisions.

3. **Benjamin Franklin**: As a founding father of the United States and a prominent figure in personal finance, Benjamin Franklin famously said, "An investment in knowledge pays the best interest."

4. "*The Intelligent Investor*" by **Benjamin Graham**: Benjamin Graham, known as the father of value investing, wrote "The Intelligent Investor," which emphasizes the importance of continuous education in personal finance. The book provides valuable insights into investment strategies, risk management, and fundamental analysis. Graham encourages investors

to approach the market with a long-term perspective, conduct thorough research, and make informed decisions based on the underlying value of the investments.

Conclusion: Continuous education about personal finance is a powerful tool for achieving economic growth, financial success, and effective management of your resources. By reading books, following experts, attending workshops, taking courses, and engaging in financial communities, you can equip yourself with the knowledge and skills to make informed decisions. Remember the wise words of Suze Orman and Benjamin Franklin, and embrace the journey of lifelong financial education. With each new lesson learned and each piece of information absorbed, you gain the confidence and competence to navigate the ever-changing financial landscape and secure a prosperous future.

Book references

Book references are presented in alphabetical order by author, with each book offering a unique perspective and actionable advice. These books empower readers to make informed financial decisions and work towards their long-term financial goals:

- Adam Grant, "*Give and Take*"
- Andrew Tobias, "*The Only Investment Guide You'll Ever Need*"
- Annie Raser-Rowland and Adam Grubb, "*The Art of Frugal Hedonism*"
- Ashley Feinstein Gerstley, "*The 30-Day Money Cleanse: Take Control of Your Finances, Manage Your Spending, and De-Stress Your Money for Good*"
- Ashton Pereira, "*Debt-Free: 9 Step System to Get Out of Debt Fast and Have Financial Freedom*"
- Benjamin Franklin, "*The Autobiography of Benjamin Franklin*"
- Benjamin Graham, "*The Intelligent Investor*"
- Bob Burg and John David Mann, "*The Go-Giver*"
- Brandon Turner and David Greene, "*The Book on Investing in Real Estate with No (and Low) Money Down*"
- Brandon Turner, "*The Book on Rental Property Investing*"
- Brian Tracy, "*Goals!: How to Get Everything You Want—Faster Than You Ever Thought Possible*"
- Burton G. Malkiel, "*A Random Walk Down Wall Street*"
- Cal Newport, "*Deep Work: Rules for Focused Success in a Distracted World*"
- Carol S. Dweck, "*Mindset: The New Psychology of Success*"
- Chris Guillebeau, "*Side Hustle: From Idea to Income in 27 Days*"
- Chris Guillebeau, "*The $100 Startup*"
- Chris Voss, "*Never Split the Difference: Negotiating As If Your Life Depended On It*"
- Dale Carnegie, "*How to Win Friends and Influence People*"
- Daniel Kahneman, "*Thinking, Fast and Slow*"
- Darren Hardy, "*The Compound Effect*"
- Dave Ramsey, "*The Total Money Makeover*"
- David Bach, "*The Automatic Millionaire: A Powerful One-Step Plan to Live and Finish Rich*"
- David Chilton, "*The Wealthy Barber*"
- Eckhart Tolle, "*The Power of Now*"
- Elizabeth Warren and Amelia Warren Tyagi, "*All Your Worth: The Ultimate Lifetime Money Plan*"
- Eric Ries, "*The Lean Startup: How Today's Entrepreneurs Use Continuous Innovation to Create Radically Successful Businesses*"
- Eric Tyson, "*Personal Finance for Dummies*"

- Ernie J. Zelinski, "*How to Retire Happy, Wild, and Free*"
- Francine Jay, "*The Joy of Less*"
- Gary Keller, Dave Jenks, and Jay Papasan, "*The Millionaire Real Estate Investor*"
- George S. Clason, "*The Richest Man in Babylon*"
- Greg McKeown, "*Essentialism: The Disciplined Pursuit of Less*"
- J.L. Collins, "*The Simple Path to Wealth*"
- Jane Bryant Quinn, "*How to Make Your Money Last*"
- Jerrold Mundis, "*Get Out of Debt, Stay Out of Debt, and Live Prosperously*"
- Jesse Mecham, "*You Need a Budget: The Proven System for Breaking the Paycheck-to-Paycheck Cycle, Getting Out of Debt, and Living the Life You Want*"
- Jim Camp, "*Start with No: The Negotiating Tools That the Pros Don't Want You to Know*"
- John C. Bogle, "*The Little Book of Common Sense Investing*"
- Josh Kaufman, "*The Personal MBA: Master the Art of Business*"
- Joshua Becker, "*The Minimalist Home*"
- Keith Ferrazzi, "*Never Eat Alone*"
- Ken McElroy, "*The ABCs of Real Estate Investing*"
- Liz Weston, "*Your Credit Score: How to Improve the 3-Digit Number That Shapes Your Financial Future*"
- Mark J. Kohler, "*The Tax and Legal Playbook*"
- Mark J. Kohler, "*What Your CPA Isn't Telling You*"
- MJ DeMarco, "*The Millionaire Fastlane*"
- Morgan Housel, "*The Psychology of Money*"
- Nassim Nicholas Taleb, "*Fooled by Randomness*"
- Nick Loper, "*The Side Hustle: How to Turn Your Spare Time into $1,000 a Month or More*"
- Peter Lynch, "*One Up On Wall Street*"
- Philip Fisher, "*Common Stocks and Uncommon Profits*"
- Ramit Sethi, "*I Will Teach You to Be Rich*"
- Ray Dalio, "*Principles: Life and Work*"
- Robert D. Manning, "*Credit Card Nation*"
- Robert G. Allen, "*Multiple Streams of Income*"
- Robert G. Hagstrom, "*The Warren Buffett Way*"
- Robert Kiyosaki, "*Rich Dad Poor Dad*"
- Robin Leonard and John Lamb, "*The Ultimate Credit Repair Guide: How to Fix, Restore, and Build Your Credit*"
- Roger Fisher, William Ury, and Bruce Patton, "*Getting to Yes: Negotiating Agreement Without Giving In*"
- Sandy Botkin, "*Lower Your Taxes - BIG TIME!*"
- Sheryl Sandberg, "*Lean In*"

- Stephen R. Covey, "*The 7 Habits of Highly Effective People*"
- Steve and Annette Economides, "*The MoneySmart Family System*"
- Steve Bucci, "*Credit Repair Kit For Dummies*"
- Suze Orman, "*The Money Book for the Young, Fabulous & Broke*"
- T. Harv Eker, "*Secrets of the Millionaire Mind*"
- Taylor Larimore, Mel Lindauer, and Michael LeBoeuf, "*The Bogleheads' Guide to Investing*"
- Taylor Larimore, Mel Lindauer, and Richard A. Ferri, "*The Bogleheads' Guide to Retirement Planning*"
- Thomas J. Stanley and William D. Danko, "*The Millionaire Next Door*"
- Timothy Ferriss, "*The 4-Hour Workweek*"
- Tom Wheelwright, "*Tax-Free Wealth*"
- Tony Robbins, "*Money: Master the Game*"
- Tony Robbins, "*Unshakeable*"
- Vicki Robin and Joe Dominguez, "*Your Money or Your Life*"
- William Bernstein, "*The Four Pillars of Investing*"

www.ingramcontent.com/pod-product-compliance
Lightning Source LLC
Chambersburg PA
CBHW052326220526
45472CB00001B/286